The Open University

Arts: A Second Level Course
Seventeenth-century England: A Changing Culture, 1618–1689

KV-579-219

Restoration Culture

Prepared for the course team by Tim Benton, Cicely Palser Havely,
Arnold Kettle, W.R. Owens and John Purkis

The Open University Press

Covers   Details from the engraved title page by Wenceslaus Hollar for John Ogilby *Britannia*, 1675. (British Museum Department of Prints and Drawings. Photograph: John R. Freeman.)

The Open University Press
Walton Hall, Milton Keynes
MK7 6AA

First published 1981

Designed by the Graphic Design Group of the Open University.

Printed in Great Britain by
Eyre & Spottiswoode Limited at Grosvenor Press, Portsmouth

ISBN 0 335 11043 6

This text forms part of an Open University course. The complete list of the course appears at the end of this text.

For general availability of supporting material referred to in this text, please write to Open University Educational Enterprises Limited, 12 Cofferidge Close, Stony Stratford, Milton Keynes, MK11 1BY, Great Britain.

Further information on Open University courses may be obtained from the Admissions Office, The Open University, PO Box 48, Walton Hall, Milton Keynes, MK7 6AB.

1.1

Block 9   Restoration Culture

Contents

Introduction to Block 9

While London burned in 1666 and during the years in which the rebuilding of the City was being planned (if that is the right word), Bunyan was in and out of jail. The Restoration culture with which this block is concerned was, in an important sense, two cultures. A juxtaposing of *The Pilgrim's Progress* with the plays and operas created for the Court tells its own tale, reminding us how little one part of the world could truly know how the other part lived.

Block 9 starts with Bunyan who, perhaps better than anyone, represents the culture of the dissenting sects. And because that culture was forged in the struggles of the sixteen-forties and fifties it is as well to begin our glance at the literature of the Restoration by reminding ourselves of that strand *least* affected (except in the sense that it came up against more rigorous repression) by the return of the Court to London in 1660.

From Bunyan we move to Dryden and Etherege but first take a glance at the phenomenon of neo-classicism which reminds us, among other things, that neither England nor its cultural developments can be isolated from the rest of Europe. Bunyan is intensely 'English' yet people like the pilgrims and townsfolk of his world were also to be found in Holland; whereas the literature of the Restoration Court links up more closely with that of Louis XIV's France.

In 'Architecture: Caroline Style and Stuart Cultural Policy' both the French and the Dutch appear a good deal. If this surprises us, recalling that between 1660 and 1688 England was at war with both countries, we have also to remember that Charles II had spent the period of the Commonwealth in France and Holland and that after 1688 the English Court was presided over by the Dutch husband of an English queen. Neo-classicism was not an 'influence' learned purely from essays and text books. It was part of the struggle to achieve a 'settlement' after 1660, a settlement which with the Glorious Revolution of 1688 and the compromises embodied in the role of William of Orange has to be seen in 'cultural' as well as 'economic' and 'political' terms.

Broadcasting

The broadcasts associated with this block consist of:
Radio programme 13, *The Office of Works*
Radio programme 14, *The Trials of Bunyan*
Television programme 13, *St Paul's Cathedral*
Television programme 14, *The Man of Mode*

Set books

You will need to use the following set books as you work through material in this block:

Christopher Hill (revised edition, 1980), *The Century of Revolution*, Nelson (*C of R*).

Ann Hughes (ed) (1980) *Seventeenth-century England: A Changing Culture*: Vol. 1, *Primary Sources*, Ward Lock (Anthology).

W. R. Owens (ed) (1980) *Seventeenth-century England: A Changing Culture*: Vol. 2, *Modern Studies*, Ward Lock (Reader).

John Bunyan (ed Roger Sharrock) (1965) *The Pilgrim's Progress*, Penguin.

Gamini Salgado (ed) (1968) *Three Restoration Comedies*, Penguin.
You will also need to refer to *Illustration Book 2*.

Cassettes

You will need to listen to the reading of *Absalom and Achitophel* on Cassette 2 (AC 206).

John Bunyan

Contents

John Bunyan

1 John Bunyan (1628–1688): a biographical introduction

In the 'Introduction' to *The Pilgrim's Progress* Professor Sharrock outlines the events of Bunyan's life; before commencing work on this section you should read at least the first five pages of Sharrock's 'Introduction'. These notes deal with two aspects of Bunyan's life: his religious conversion, and his work as a sectarian preacher and writer. They should help you to place Bunyan in the changing culture which you have been studying, and also to relate *The Pilgrim's Progress* to Bunyan's experiences and to the society in which he lived. All references to *The Pilgrim's Progress* are to the 1965 Penguin edition.

Religious conversion

In 1666 Bunyan published a spiritual autobiography, *Grace Abounding to the Chief of Sinners* (*GA*), relating in vivid detail the story of 'the work of God upon my own soul' (*GA*, pp 1–2). You have worked on other examples of sectarian autobiography in Block 4, and *Grace Abounding* is similar to these in form and content. Bunyan's conviction that he was a sinful creature who needed God's forgiveness was aroused by reading Puritan books belonging to his first wife. For a while he tried to reform his life, giving up swearing, drinking, Sunday sport, even bell-ringing which he so much enjoyed, but still he remained oppressed by guilt and fear. One day he overheard in the street in Bedford 'three or four poor women sitting at a door in the sun, and talking about the things of God'. Bunyan was 'greatly affected': 'me thought they spake as if joy did make them speak . . . they were to me as if they had found a new world' (*GA*, pp 14–15). In his quest for spiritual enlightenment he talked with Ranters and Quakers, read their books, and began to study the Bible, searching desperately for verses which would assure him of salvation, but often finding ones which, to his despair, seemed to condemn him. He met John Gifford, pastor of the little separatist church in Bedford to which the 'poor women' belonged, and was greatly helped by his advice on spiritual matters. (Gifford was probably the model for Evangelist in *The Pilgrim's Progress*.) For Bunyan, however, it took years of psychological struggle, during which he swung from moods of despondency to moments of ecstatic vision, before he could feel confident that he was indeed an elect child of God.

His greatest crisis came when he believed that he had succumbed to the devil's temptation to 'sell and part with Christ' (*GA*, p 43). For almost two years the doubt and despair which gripped him was so intense that he felt at times 'such a clogging and heat at my stomach . . . as if my breast-bone would have split in sunder'. 'Thus did I wind, and twine, and shrink under the burden that was upon me; which burden did so oppress me, that I could neither stand nor go, nor lie either at rest or quiet' (*GA*, p 50). Gradually, as he searched and pondered the scriptures, he came to believe that he had not after all committed the unpardonable sin: 'Now did my chains fall off my legs indeed, I was loosed from my affliction and irons, my temptations also fled away' (*GA*, p 72).

About 1655 Bunyan joined the Bedford congregation, and was baptized by immersion. About two years later he began to preach publically. His preaching drew upon his own experience: 'I preached what I felt, what I smartingly did feel' (*GA*, p 85). Likewise, *The Pilgrim's Progress* grew out of *Grace Abounding*.

John Bunyan

Sectarian preacher and writer

In common with other sectarian preachers, Bunyan suffered attacks by the regular clergy, who thought that allowing unlearned and unordained men to preach would undermine the whole social fabric. As Thomas Hall put it, 'Superiors must govern, inferiors obey, and be governed. Ministers must study and preach, people must hear and obey' (see *Anthology*, Extract 71). Bunyan was acutely aware of his humble social status, but he defended his right to preach vigorously against the contempt of the established authorities. He remarked that Christ 'earned his bread with his labour, being by trade a carpenter' (*The Works of John Bunyan*, Vol I, p 345). As for the learning of university-trained clerics: 'I tell you that the operation of the Word and Spirit of God, without depending on that idol [learning], so much adored, is sufficient of itself to search out "all things, even the deep things of God" ' (*The Works of John Bunyan*, Vol III, p 397).

Bunyan's class consciousness and antagonism towards his social superiors is clearly, though not always consistently, evidenced in many of his works. There was nothing 'theoretic' about his class sympathies; it was simply that in Bunyan's experience, the enemies of the aspiring saints were in fact the rich and powerful. In an early work he interpreted the parable of Dives and Lazarus (Luke 16): 'the beggar holdeth forth the godly, and the rich man the ungodly'. Running throughout this work is a strong current of resentment against the pride and covetousness of the rich and their oppression of the poor and defenceless:

> how many pounds do some men spend in a year on their dogs, when in the meanwhile the poor saints of God may starve for hunger? . . . And if they be in any of their houses for the hire thereof, they will warn them out or eject them, or pull down the house over their heads, rather than not rid themselves of such tenants.
>
> (*The Works of John Bunyan*, Vol III, pp 676, 677.)

Elsewhere Bunyan declared that heaven 'is prepared for the poor': 'I am apt to think sometimes, that more servants than masters, that more tenants than landlords, will inherit the kingdom of heaven' (*The Works of John Bunyan*, Vol III, pp 390, 394). In *The Pilgrim's Progress*, you will observe that the ungodly are of the gentry or nobility (e.g. pp 47, 131, 136), while pilgrims are from the lower classes (e.g. pp 86, 106–8).

As an itinerant preacher Bunyan frequently took part in theological controversies, both verbal and written. His first published works were polemics against the Quakers. Later he wrote against the latitudinarian, Edward Fowler, and became involved in doctrinal disputes with a number of London Baptists. These controversies were conducted in seventeenth-century fashion, including rancorous personal abuse on each side, and, as notes to your set book indicate (pp 375–7), Bunyan clearly had some of his opponents in mind when writing *The Pilgrim's Progress*.

In all these activities and attitudes Bunyan was a typical 'mechanick' preacher, resembling a host of others who exercised their gifts under the Commonwealth (see accounts of the sects in Blocks 4, 6 and 8). With the Restoration the comparative freedom which had existed under Cromwell came to an end. Bunyan was one of the first nonconformists to suffer. His judges were Royalists who were determined to put the tinker back in his place; and you will hear Bunyan's account of his trial in Radio Programme 14. But their attempt to silence Bunyan gave him instead the impetus imaginatively to transmute his experiences into a great work of literary art, one which provides revealing insights into seventeenth-century Puritanism and the society in which it flourished.

2 Reading Bunyan

> 'There was some books too . . . One was a big family Bible, full of pictures. One was *Pilgrim's Progress*, about a man that left his family it didn't say why. I read considerable in it now and then. The statements was interesting, but tough.'
>
> (*Huckleberry Finn*, 1884, Penguin ed. p 159)

In one respect at least Huck Finn was right. *The Pilgrim's Progress* is a tough book. Its capacity to survive tells us that. But for the modern reader it can also be tough in a different way, tough to come to terms with as a literary text.

Rather than beginning with a fairly general and theoretical discussion of possible approaches, let us plunge straight into the opening pages and discover what actual problems occur. I shall concentrate in this section on the very first paragraph; but in order to get that into some sort of context and perspective, please read the first six pages (pp 39–45), up to the point at which Pliable turns back, leaving Christian in the Slough of Despond.

EXERCISE

Precisely how are we to take these phrases:

(a) The wilderness of this world

(b) A den

(c) I dreamed a dream

(d) a book in his hand, and a great burden upon his back

(e) What shall I do?

DISCUSSION

(a) Bunyan isn't saying that the world is *like* a wilderness, but that it *is* a wilderness. The difference may not seem very significant, but in fact I think it is. It has often been remarked that these opening words of *The Pilgrim's Progress* bear a striking similarity to the opening of Dante's *Inferno*, the first part of *The Divine Comedy*, the most famous of all mediaeval religious poems, which begins 'In the middle of the journey of our life I came to myself in a dark wood where the straight way was lost'. This is enough to remind us that *The Pilgrim's Progress*, though a unique book and certainly very different from Dante, is written within a tradition, that of Christian allegory.

An allegory is a story in the form of an extended metaphor in which a concept like 'journey' or 'progress' is used to 'stand for' something other than its first or normal meaning. All imaginative writing uses metaphor to some extent. But allegory is an extreme form of metaphorical writing. It is more than a literary convention. There seems to be implied in it that the surface meaning (the first 'leg' of the metaphor, so to speak) is less important, indeed less 'real' or 'true', than the hidden meaning: and one tends in consequence to get the sense that the hidden meaning or 'message' exists in the writer's mind prior to the particular expression the story takes and to treat the story therefore as an illustration rather than an exploration. Thus *The Pilgrim's Progress* may appear to be about a journey but is 'really' about salvation, and the world (i.e. our world of fallen men) is *really* a wilderness.

There is, however, a danger in treating allegory in this way, as though the allegorist were only interested in general and abstract ideas. In one sense it's true enough to say that Bunyan's Pilgrim with his burden on his back 'stands for' or illustrates fallen man and that his Progress 'stands for' the achievement of salvation. But putting it that way shows a certain insensitiveness to language and can in practice take the guts out of the book. For the very words pilgrim and progress are not mere abstractions but have a flesh-and-blood, specific historical reality, which absorbs change as well as tradition. Bunyan's Christian is not at all like the mediaeval knights who made a pilgrimage to the Holy Land and his progress is not at all like the progresses the kings and queens of England made through their country from one great house to another. The very words Bunyan uses emerge out of the life he led as well as out of their traditional uses and associations. So that when we come upon a phrase like 'the wilderness of this world' we have, I think, to read it in a double way. We are conscious that it *evokes* the whole Christian concept of the world which fallen man inhabits after being driven from Eden and the *reality* of which to seventeenth-century Puritans was embodied in the Bible itself: and *at the same time* we are also conscious that it is what the world looks and feels like to an individual man or woman in the midst of an acute personal psychological crisis. In other words, Bunyan, like every fine writer, transforms words as he uses them and the transformation emerges out of the way he grapples with experience (which included, of course, his thoughts). To say that *The Pilgrim's Progress* is about sin and salvation and to leave it at that is not only an inadequate way of describing its content: it has the further danger of suggesting that if you, the reader, don't go along with the Christian doctrine you aren't likely to be able to go along with the book.

(b)   We know the den is a gaol because of Bunyan's marginal note. The interesting question is why he should have added this in the third edition. Presumably it is because the den, though it reinforces the image of the wilderness, isn't – like the wilderness itself – an essential part of the allegory as such. And for some reason it suits Bunyan's purposes better to link it with the actual world he lived in, the prison at Bedford, and his own status as struggling and obstinate human being, rather than to incorporate it fully into the allegorical meaning of the book. This strikes me as important because it asserts from the start a certain contradiction – or, at least, a tension – deep in *The Pilgrim's Progress* and in Bunyan's attitude to it. On the one hand it's an allegory asserting the prime reality of a religious view embodied in a supreme confidence in a world which is to come: on the other (and at the same time) it is a very specific and concrete product of *this* world at a particular moment in its history.

(c)   Since we already know from the title page of *The Pilgrim's Progress* that it is 'delivered under the Similitude of a Dream', we realize that Bunyan's chief purpose here must be to stress the status of the dream as, first and foremost, a literary convention. The story that follows is neither more or less 'true' because it is a dream. Bunyan needs some such convention because otherwise his book will be either too simply realistic (because insufficiently 'inward') or else too remote from this world (and hence insufficiently urgent as a guide to action). And his full awareness of what he was doing is shown – among other ways – by the way he returns to the question of the dream in the 'Conclusion' of Part I (p 205). It is a good example of his sure instinct as an artist (of which more later, pp 15–16).

(d)   Whether we recognize that the book the man is carrying is likely to be the Bible and the burden sin will depend not just on careful reading but on how familiar we are with Christian theology, seventeenth-century habits of mind (cf. Block 1 'A Different World From Ours') and the allegorical tradition in literature. If, like Huckleberry Finn, we haven't quite grasped the idea of Original Sin, we are unlikely to cotton on immediately to the point of the burden and may wonder why the man is so upset. But if we bring to the book a certain effort of historical imagination, there is no great problem, for we will be prepared for such resonances. Whether or not we ourselves 'believe in' the notion of Original Sin isn't of key importance as long as our minds are open to the *force* of Christian's obsessions. The importance of seeing *The Pilgrim's Progress* in history springs less from the need for a detailed knowledge of the historical background than from a general awareness of the sort of changes and conflicts of ideas going on in seventeenth-century England.

(e)   The heartfelt cry 'What shall I do?' through its tone and urgency establishes beyond doubt that this religious allegory – based in one sense on a theological dogma – is centrally concerned with specific concrete human dilemmas and actions. It is true that there is a Calvinist theology (cf. Sharrock's 'Introduction', p 18) a system of ideas, behind the book and therefore a sense in which it is an illustration of an existing doctrine; but it isn't a doctrinaire or abstracted Calvinism that strikes at the reader's heart and mind when we hear Christian's cry. It is an actual human situation, a man in deep agony of mind, not knowing where to turn: the sort of situation a realist novelist might offer us.

I have dwelt on that first paragraph because an examination of it brings out, it seems to me, at least five important general aspects of *The Pilgrim's Progress*. To summarize them

(a)   It is an allegory.

(b)   It has an important autobiographical element to it.

(c)   It is a work of literary art.

(d)   It belongs to and has to be seen in the light of seventeenth-century history.

(e)   It is deeply impregnated with realism.

3   Allegory and realism

Let us examine a little further my suggestion that there lies deep within Bunyan's conception of *The Pilgrim's Progress* a certain tension between the *allegorical* conception of the book and its *realism*.[1] But before you proceed any further into this discussion it's essential that you should have read the whole of *The Pilgrim's Progress,* or at least Part I, from which I will take some examples.

The Valley of the Shadow of Death (pp 95–101)

It would be hard to find a more fully allegorical and non–realist passage than this. Its whole power and effect depends on the sense it evokes of the danger and closeness of Hell and upon traditional imagery, as when the men (the children of the spies, see Numbers 3:32), making haste to go back, describe the Valley with its hobgoblins, satyrs, dragons and 'continual howling and yelling, as of a people under unutterable misery who sat there bound in affliction and irons' (p 96).

Yet even such a passage seems to work (as far as the reader is concerned) through a mixture of allegorical and directly realist effects. Try making a list of the elements which could be called 'realist'.

I will pick out a few (which may well be different from yours for there are many to choose from).

(a)   The colloquial nature of the dialogue between Christian and the children of the spies, based not on traditional or Biblical imagery but on actual speech. For example '"Why? what's the matter?" said Christian. "Matter!"

---

[1]I use the words 'realism' and 'realist' in these pages very cagily (hence the inverted commas) for they are complex and nearly always ambiguous words. Chiefly I am using them to contrast two literary conventions – the 'allegorical' (e.g. as in *The Pilgrim's Progress*) and the 'realist' (e.g. as in *Moll Flanders* or *Jane Eyre*); but it is a contrast that can't be limited to literary conventions. The whole problem of the use and implications of the words 'real' and 'really' is involved and this introduces linguistic and philosophical difficulties which can neither be ignored nor usefully over-simplified.

said they' (p 95), or '"But what have you seen?" said Christian. "Seen! Why the Valley itself, which is as dark as pitch"' (p 96). 'The vigour of Bunyan's prose is more than a matter of an earthy raciness that consorts happily with biblical turns and resonances' F. R. Leavis has rightly said (Sharrock *The Pilgrim's Progress: A Selection of Critical Essays,* p 212). It is fed by the quality of experience and struggle that get into it.

(b)   The physical description of Christian walking along the path in the dark: 'the pathway was here so dark that oft times when he lift up his foot to set forward he knew not where, or upon what, he should set it next' (p 97).

(c)   A phrase like 'sometimes he had half a thought to go back' (p 97).

(d)   The first paragraph of p 98 beginning 'One thing I would not let slip . . .' This is described by Bunyan in the marginal note in entirely non-realist terms, with Satan playing the key-role. Yet what emerges is a psychological experience of great force and realism: the sense of hearing oneself say things that one does not fully understand or even want to say.

(e)   The episode (pp 100–1) in which, emerging from the Valley, Christian comes up with, overtakes and is finally helped up by Faithful: 'Then I saw in my dream they went very lovingly on together, and had sweet discourse of all things that had happened to them in their pilgrimage . . .' The sense here is of the need and importance of human community. Though each pilgrim has to meet certain tests and trials alone, the result is to strengthen mutual fellowship. And this result is conveyed not in the abstract terms of allegorical significance but in a vibrant sense of human interdependence and mutual need.

Vanity Fair

The Vanity Fair episode is central to *The Pilgrim's Progress.* Not only does the trial of Christian and Faithful echo Bunyan's own trial; what the pilgrims find that they are up against is not merely intolerance, repression and ideas turned upside down (so that Beelzebub is Prince and the Judge is Hategood), but a *culture.*

The culture of Vanity Fair is cosmopolitan, trivial, tawdry: essentially it is based on commerce; everything is merchandise, including wives, husbands and children as well as houses, lands, titles etc. The link between this kind of market and certain debased forms of pilgrimage is one which may well strike the twentieth-century reader; anyone who has visited Mont St Michel on the coast of Brittany, once the scene of religious pilgrimages, will know what I mean. We are reminded that even in the Middle Ages pilgrimage had its tourist aspects.

The major problem for Bunyan's pilgrims is to resist assimilation and maintain at all costs their confidence that they will overcome. For this they need all the resources of their alternative culture. They dress, talk and act differently from the men of the Fair. It is not just a question of abstract ideas but of two ways of life that are in conflict. To recognize this situation is to recognize some of the central problems of Bunyan as a writer. There is a point beyond which he feels he dare not compromise. If we complain that to give a judge a name like Hategood is to weight the scales of language as well as justice beyond plausibility, he could well reply that the pilgrims have nothing to protect themselves with beyond their own refusal to sell the truth and their sense of the necessity of holding together a culture involving totally different values. The question of language is in itself an interesting one and has been touched on in Block 2 (pp 84–5) in the distinction between 'witty' (i.e. sophisticated) and 'plain' speech. Bunyan is a 'plain' speaker in the tradition of the Puritan preachers, but that word doesn't imply a lack of art. When he says of the pilgrims 'they naturally spoke the language of Canaan; but they that kept the Fair, were the men of this world; so that from one end of the Fair to the other, they seemed barbarians each to the other' he is at the same time using the language of allegory (for obviously he doesn't mean that the pilgrims literally spoke a different language) and making an acute social observation about class and cultural divisions.

The *isolation* of the pilgrims in Vanity Fair is indicative of one of the problems of the seventeenth-century Puritan sects (especially after 1660) and also, I think, raises a problem of response for a considerable proportion of twentieth-century readers. How are we to respond to the pilgrims' conviction of being a chosen elect, seventeenth-century children of Israel, sometimes passive and even quiescent and falling back upon their sense of 'difference' from the mass of mankind? How are we to respond to the intense sectarianism of the sects themselves?

The cultural forms of expression chosen and developed by small minority groups battling – sometimes against the strongest opposition and in the face of very real danger – against the dominant forces of the day are likely to reflect the fears and obsessions of such minorities. The cage in which Christian and Faithful are imprisoned, was not, after all, a mere symbol of an abstract oppression. And it is worth comparing the culture of the nonconforming, often persecuted sects of the late seventeenth century (or, for that matter, the earlier Puritan communities who decided to emigrate to America) with that of the black people of the United States who have drawn so much strength from the songs that came to be known as spirituals and were themselves, ironically, a transmuted inheritance from the culture of their masters. When Bunyan wrote in the Preface to *Grace Abounding*

> My Dear Children,
> The Milk and Honey is beyond this Wilderness: God be merciful to you, and grant that you be not slothful to go in to possess the Land,

he wasn't offering his flock pie in the sky any more than the black slaves and their descendants who sang

> Go down Moses, way down in Egypt's land.
> Tell old Pharaoh: Let my people go

were running away from their world to a never-never land represented by ancient Egypt. In both cases what the artist is offering and the people responding to is a call to overcome intolerable burdens through determination, solidarity and struggle. Possessing the land is in one sense a dream of the future, but it is a dream that keeps hope and therefore struggle alive. Allegory can in this sense be thought of as capable of deep realism.

Puritan literature in the seventeenth century sometimes gives the sense of being extremely inward-turned. This corresponds with the isolation of the sects and their need for a firm inner resolve. It was when the nonconformists began to become more powerful, economically and politically, that they developed a more relaxed, outgoing and 'realist' style of writing, forged in enterprise and activity of a practical nature. This development is discussed in my article on 'Puritanism and the Rise of the Novel' (reprinted in the Reader, article 25). You may find it useful to consider *The Pilgrim's Progress* within the context of the development of the realist novel. Bunyan died in 1688, the year of the Glorious Revolution. Defoe was born in 1660, the year of the Restoration. *The Pilgrim's Progress* was published in 1678, while Defoe was attending a Dissenting Academy and considering becoming, like Bunyan, a nonconforming minister. Defoe was to become, in fact, a businessman and journalist and, within thirty years of the Revolution of 1688, a realist novelist, author of *Robinson Crusoe* and *Moll Flanders*. To take the story into the nineteenth century, another novelist, Thackeray, a conscious 'realist', published in 1848, another year of revolutions, a novel of social criticism which he called *Vanity Fair*.

The naming of characters

For many people the decisive factor which enables them to recognize an allegory when they see one is the naming of characters. We know *The Pilgrim's Progress* is an allegory because the characters have names like Christ-

John Bunyan

ian, Faithful, Hopeful, Mr Worldly-Wiseman, By-Ends and so on. The implication is usually taken to be that the people in the book are simply personifications of abstract ideas or qualities. Further implications are likely to be that they are lacking true individuality and are therefore not very 'real' and that the whole project of which they are a part is inevitably a gross, if worthy, over-simplification of life as a whole.

EXERCISE

Obviously, with limited time and space, we can't enter into a very deep consideration of such problems. But I would like you to be thinking about (and making notes on) the following questions:

(a)   Is it reasonable to expect any character in fiction not to be presented in a simplified and to some extent allegorical way?

(b)   How would you compare Bunyan's naming of his characters with that of such figures as Guardiano and Sordido (*Women Beware Women*), Sir Fopling Flutter (*The Man of Mode*), Lycidas. (If you have read the books concerned you might care to add Squire Allworthy from *Tom Jones* and the characters of Thackeray's *Vanity Fair* to your list.)

DISCUSSION

(a)   This question, as you'll no doubt have realized, is intended to act as a warning that the whole problem of the naming and nature of fictional characters is, like the whole relationship of allegory and realism, much more complex and diffficult than one might think.

No character in fiction is 'real': the most that can be said of him or her is that he or she is 'convincing' or gives the reader the sense of having something real or true or recognizable or revelatory or at least interesting about him (her).

All fictional characters serve a purpose thought out, more or less consistently, by their author. They are inevitably presented in ways suited to those purposes. In this sense all characters are functional: it is only when their function is crudely or boringly obvious or banal that we need to complain.

The characters in *The Pilgrim's Progress* are presented, not quite as embodiments of a single abstract quality, but as types associated with particular characteristics and activities. It has been noticed that their names are more often adjectival (i.e. Faithful, Hopeful etc) than substantive (i.e. Shame, Mercy) in form. We tend nowadays, perhaps, to see types and individuals as quite different, and indeed opposing, categories, so that when a critic describes a character in a novel or play as a type, this tends to be taken as a hostile comment, indicating a crude approach. But in fact to see individual and type as opposites is itself a crudification of a much more complex relationship. Shakespeare's Hamlet – everyone agrees – is a most subtle, complex and individual figure: yet he is also presented as a type, well-established in Elizabethan drama and life – 'the melancholy man'. Shakespeare's audience would recognize him as 'one of those' before becoming aware of his full complexity.

Clearly the characters in *The Pilgrim's Progress* are presented as types, the Pilgrim himself included, and, unlike Hamlet, their more detailed psychological and intellectual complexities are not explored. The important question is: does this make them less convincingly real, or individual as fictional characters? If our instinct is to reject the convincingness of Bunyan's fictional characters *because* they are types and therefore not individuals, then I think we have to do a bit more thinking, not only about literary conventions but also about ourselves and the relation of the individual to the society of which he is a part. Perhaps a reference back to the discussion on metaphysical poetry in Block 2 might be relevant.

(b)   The whole business of naming characters in fictional works is indeed more complicated than we are apt to realize. Middleton (like Shakespeare) gives his central characters more or less neutral names though they are frequently not without metaphorical undertones (e.g. Bottom, Falstaff, Prospero). Sordido and Guardiano – minor characters – are not of the greatest relevance or interest and can therefore be given functional names which are a kind of shorthand to help the audience to recognize them and their (limited) roles in the play. The convention in Etherege is rather different. Nearly all the characters, not just Sir Fopling, are given names which connect them with types and exaggerate a single characteristic. This convention is linked with the crude, but widely accepted, mediaeval notion that individuals were composed of various elements (blood, phlegm, bile etc) which, mixed in differing quantities, produced differing psychological temperaments or 'humours' (e.g. the use of such words as sanguine, phlegmatic etc.). But a writer didn't necessarily have to swallow the entire 'humours' theory to recognize that to stress one particular characteristic of a person can be an effective and economical way of presenting him or her on the stage or in a tale, thereby easily distinguishing one character from another and at the same time indicating significant patterns in the work. As for Lycidas, this is a conventional name in the purest sense, and doesn't have much relevance to *The Pilgrim's Progress* except to remind us that Bunyan is working in a convention more 'realistic' than that.

(Squire Allworthy in *Tom Jones* (who lives in Paradise Hall) is a character who owes a good deal to allegory in his presentation. The characters in *Vanity Fair* are not overtly allegorical – though names like Becky Sharp and Dobbin have a metaphorical undertone – but it's interesting that Thackeray often refers to them as 'puppets', stressing their functional or representative role within his total 'realist' creation.)

4 'The Pilgrim's Progress' as literary art

One of the main objects of these pages on Bunyan has been to discuss what it is that makes *The Pilgrim's Progress* not simply an interesting historical document or a tract with an inspired message for believers, but a book that can engage and move a modern reader, whatever his religious or non-religious beliefs.

Roger Sharrock in his Introduction (p 24) to the set book answers the question by suggesting that what 'gives the work its continuing vitality is the creation, not of allegory, but of myth'. The problem with such an answer is that the word 'myth' involves as many ambiguities and difficulties as the word 'allegory' and is used by different scholars and critics in widely differing ways, including some highly idiosyncratic (not to say unscientific) ones.

The important point, I'd suggest, if we are to arrive at a reasonably objective way of discussing such a problem is to avoid, on the one hand (a) formulations which *reduce* Bunyan's book by attempting to 'translate' it into less challenging terms (e.g. to suggest that Bunyan didn't 'really' mean that men and women acquired eternal life through achieving salvation), and (b) unhistorical abstractions in which the concreteness and force of Bunyan's metaphors are lost.

If we use the word 'art' or the phrase 'a work of literary art' about *The Pilgrim's Progress* (and for myself I can see no better way of describing the nature of its power), this is not to imply that 'art' or 'literature' are mystical or autonomous categories above or beyond time and space. Even in the three hundred years since Bunyan lived the word 'art' has greatly changed its connotations and resonances. Neither Bunyan himself nor the following generations who read and treasured his book normally thought of him as an artist.

Yet to return (for instance) to the 'Apology' printed at the beginning of the text (pp 31–7) is to realize how conscious he was of the preoccupations and problems which have concerned creative artists of many different kinds and eras.

> I only thought to make
> I knew not what, nor did I undertake
> Thereby to please my neighbour; no, not I,
> I did it mine own self to gratify . . .

What one has here is a sense of (a) writing as a form of experiment and exploration in which the writer only discovers in the course of his practice precisely what it is he is trying to say; (b) writing that 'pleases', i.e. communicates through a shared enjoyment and vitality; and (c) writing which is produced not for a market but from a conviction of its own intrinsic value and importance.

Obviously the word 'intrinsic' in the last sentence has to be used with care. It does not imply that artistic or aesthetic value is a wholly separable category with its own fully autonomous existence and criteria. Bunyan was no art-for-art's-sake aesthete. Like Milton he saw no contradiction between writing for his 'own self' and justifying the ways of God. If we are to call Bunyan a great literary artist (as I think we must) we need a definition of literary art which includes recognition of both its uniqueness *and* its representative quality. If we see either literature or ourselves as somehow outside or beyond history we shall find it hard to 'enjoy' and 'explain' *The Pilgrim's Progress*.

References

Bunyan, John (ed Roger Sharrock) (1962) *Grace Abounding to the Chief of Sinners*, Oxford University Press.

Bunyan, John, (ed Roger Sharrock) (1965) *The Pilgrim's Progress*, Penguin. (Set Book).

The Works of John Bunyan, ed. George Offor (1860–2) 3 vols., London and Edinburgh.

Owens, W. R. (ed) (1980) *Seventeenth-century England: A Changing Culture*, Vol 2, Modern Studies, Ward Lock (Reader).

Sharrock, Roger (ed) (1976) *The Pilgrim's Progress: A Selection of Critical Essays*, Macmillan Casebook.

Further reading

Vincent Newey (ed) (1980) *The Pilgrim's Progress: Critical and Historical Views*, Liverpool University Press.

Roger Sharrock (1968) *John Bunyan*, Macmillan.

Roger Sharrock (ed) (1976) *The Pilgrim's Progress: A Selection of Critical Essays*, Macmillan Casebook.

W. Y. Tindall (1934, reprinted 1964) *John Bunyan, Mechanick Preacher*, Columbia University Press.

Alick West (1958) 'John Bunyan' in *The Mountain in the Sunlight*, Lawrence & Wishart; reprinted (1975) in *Crisis and Criticism and Selected Literary Essays*, Lawrence & Wishart.

Restoration Culture and Neo-classicism

Contents

Restoration Culture and Neo-classicism

1 Introductory

'Cardinal Richelieu', wrote Richard Flecknoe in his *Short Discourse on the English Stage,* was 'the first that brought [heroic plays] into Vogue and Esteem as now they are; well knowing how much the Acting noble and heroick Playes conferr'd to the instilling a noble and heroic Spirit into the Nation'. Flecknoe was writing in 1664, four years after the Restoration and in the same essay he goes out of his way to praise Charles II because 'after his happy Restauration he took such care to purge [the Stage] of all vice and debauchery'.

Flecknoe's words remind us of two facts: (a) that with the Restoration began a certain vogue for plays described as 'heroic tragedies', of which Dryden's *The Conquest of Granada* (an excerpt from which is included in the Anthology, extract 133) is an example, and (b) that the encouragement of such literature was part of a specific policy towards the arts which had its origins in seventeenth-century France.

The main aims of this short section are to draw your attention to (i) the sort of culture that many of those who carried through and supported the Restoration settlement wanted to encourage or impose, (ii) some of the difficulties experienced in attempts to follow the French example in such matters and (iii) the lasting significance of neo-classicism in post-Restoration culture.

I should make clear that it is, above all, a *literary* culture that I am referring to, including the drama; but I believe the issues raised have a wider, more general application.

The context of the cultural developments and policies to which I shall refer has already been indicated by Professor J. R. Jones in Block 8 'From the Restoration to the Revolution of 1688'. One of Professor Jones's themes is that while 'superficially the Restoration and the subsequent settlement did seem to achieve a return to the old order that had been destroyed after 1642', in fact the restored ruling class was not able to fulfil many of its more reactionary aims, that it was, indeed, a *different* ruling class and that although an attempt was made to reverse the attitudes to authority that had developed in the forties and fifties, in fact it proved impossible to put the clock back. It is the *cultural* implications of this situation – also dealt with in Part Three of *C of R* (especially p 208ff) – that I am concerned with in these few pages.

2 The French example

Not only Charles II but many of his supporters had spent a considerable time in France and were well aware of the development of a vast and ambitious Court culture, centred on Versailles, under Louis XIV. This culture was not only hierarchical and nationalist (i.e. bound up with the achievement of a centralized national monarchy), with a special emphasis on 'la gloire', but also very self-consciously 'classical', attempting to learn and gain prestige from the classical past, especially the drama and epics of the Greeks and the splendours of Augustan Rome. It was a culture deliberately fostered by Richelieu and Louis XIV as part of a political policy and the founding of the French Academy was an important aspect of it. For example, D'Antignac, one of the leading neo-classical critics, in his *Pratique du Théatre,* begun in 1640, clearly stated the view that, the French character being heroic and serious, the French public was inclined to regard the adventures of heroes sympathetically. Stories of horror and extraordinary cruelty were no longer acceptable, nor were recitals of kings in misery and noble families cast down, since the French nation had too much respect for their kings and princes to view such horrors with equanimity (see T. Burnley-Jones and B. de Bear Nicol, *Neo-Classical Dramatic Criticism 1560–1770*, p 64). As Irène Simon puts it:

> Through the Academy, as through his home policy, Richelieu was setting his house in order and putting an end to the lawlessness of the earlier seventeenth century; as he was marshalling all the forces of his grand design, so the literary critics were teaching genius to serve under nature and reason.
>
> (*Neo Classical Criticism 1660–1800*, p 11)

You will recall from your work on Block 2 comparable developments in early Stuart drama, though the French were much stronger on 'theory' than the British in the earlier part of the century. By the sixteen-fifties, however, British political and literary theorists and practitioners with a knowledge of the French Court – Cowley, Davenant and Hobbes are examples – were basing their defence of poetry on arguments closely comparable to those of the French neo-classicists. Hobbes, in 1650, was already defending 'heroic poetry' on direct socio-political grounds, and it is interesting to compare and contrast his attitude to the epic with Milton's (see Block 7):

> As Philosophers have divided the Universe, their subject, into three Regions, Celestiall, Aeriall, and Terrestriall, so the Poets (whose work it is, by imitating humane life in delightful and measur'd lines, to avert men from vice and incline them to vertuous and honorable actions) have lodged themselves in the three Regions of mankinde, *Court, City* and *Country*, correspondent in some proportion to those three Regions of the world. For there is in Princes and men of conspicuous power, anciently called Heroes, a lustre and influence upon the rest of men resembling that of the Heavens; and an insincereness, inconstancy and troublesome humor of those that dwell in populous Cities, like the mobility, blustering, and impurity of the Aire; and a plainness, and, though dull, yet a nutritive faculty in rurall people, that endures a comparison with the Earth they labour. From hence have proceeded three sorts of Poesy, Heroique, Scommatique [satiric], and Pastoral . . .
>
> (Spingarn (ed) *Critical Essays of the Seventeenth Century*, pp 54–5.)

The mixture in Hobbes of mediaeval scholastic notions, neo-classical aesthetics, authoritarian politics and modern materialist philosophy is particularly fascinating.

The attempt after 1660 to follow Richelieu's example and crowd the British stage with plays in which the principal object was – in the name of nature and reason – to excite admiration for an idealized version of the heroic virtues of the leaders of the nation did indeed result in dozens of heroic tragedies. Such plays were welcomed by establishment critics as vastly superior to the products of the Elizabethan and Jacobean stage. Shakespeare was generally held to be a remarkable writer, but unfortunately barbarous, strong on 'nature' but lacking in 'wit' and with little sense of decorum. Restoration Tragedy was (as Bonamy Dobrée reminds us) 'primarily a courtly art, written for the King's Players, or the Duke of York's Players, to act before fashionable audiences, and not meant for the groundlings of the Phoenix or Globe' (*Restoration Tragedy*, p 18).

Yet even with such an audience the campaign for 'heroic tragedy' had, even in the short run, only a limited success. Contemporary comments often accuse the audiences of laughing in the wrong places, and even the conservative Flecknoe (see above p 18) could say that 'Our theatres now for cost and ornament are arrived to the heighth of magnificence; but that which makes our stage the better makes our plays the worse perhaps, they striving now to make them more for sight than hearing.'

EXERCISE

Why, would you suppose, did this attempt of the Restoration Court to learn from the glamorous example of the French not really succeed? Jot down a few suggestions.

DISCUSSION

Here are some points:

(a)   However much Charles II and his entourage may have desired to import a culture from Versailles and despite the closeness of France referred to by J. R. Jones (Reader, article 4), the French connection was not really a very well-founded or popular one. For example
(i) Anti-Catholic feeling persisted.
(ii) Within a few years of the Restoration England was at war with France.
(iii) Many people believed that the French, along with the Dutch, were responsible for almost every current threat and calamity, such as the Great Fire of 1666.

(b)   The most common view of the French, even among the upper classes and reflected in dozens of Restoration comedies, was that they were affected, effeminate and figures of fun. *The Man of Mode* is a good example. Sir Fopling Flutter arrives 'piping hot from Paris' and gives his servants French names; the more French he becomes the sillier he sounds.

(c)   Most fundamental of all, Restoration England and its culture was basically very different from seventeenth-century France. The Restoration brought the monarchy back, but on the basis of a compromise which could not obliterate the previous twenty years. The civil wars and the Revolution had changed everything. Neither Charles II nor his supporters were in any position to impose a thorough-going authoritarian culture on the country, much as they may have wished to.

3   Neo-classicism

The great heroic epic of the 1660–88 period was, as we know, *Paradise Lost*. But Milton's epic cannot be seen by any stretch of the imagination as promoting the values which supporters of the Restoration settlement wished to encourage. It was not the kind of thing Cardinal Richelieu or Thomas Hobbes or Richard Flecknoe had in mind at all when *they* spoke of the virtues of heroic poetry.

   That is not to say that French literary theory and practice had no lasting influence on post-Restoration culture; but rather that this influence took a subtler and more flexible form. If you compare Dryden's plays with Shakespeare's or his poems with Milton's or the Metaphysicals', and also recognize what a strong influence he was to have on eighteenth-century Augustan poetry, you will understand what I am driving at. Dryden is a neo-classicist. Neo-classicism, in the wide sense of the term, received its greatest stimulation from the French Academy; and neo-classicism was to be the important new strain in English post-Restoration literary culture.

   Neo-classicism: it's a dry, academic term and can easily be a misleading and off-putting one. It doesn't mean simply respect for the culture of the Greeks and Romans: the Elizabethans had had plenty of that, and *Paradise Lost* is as saturated with classical reference as Dryden's poetry. The peculiar quality of neo-classicism is that it identifies the 'classical' virtues with the general social values which the ruling classes of seventeenth-century France and post-Restoration England wished to encourage and thought of as particularly civilized. Geoffrey Tillotson puts it this way:

> Wordsworth thought of the poet as a 'man speaking to men'. Clearly this is the implied view of all poets who publish their poems. Much therefore depends on what is meant by 'man' and what by 'men'. If

the poets of the late seventeenth and early eighteenth centuries had used the phrase, as they might well have done, they would have meant by 'man' the poet in his capacity as member of a civilized society, and by 'men' those other members of it who resembled him in everthing but poetic gifts.

(Tillotson, *Augustan Poetic Diction*, pp 13–14.)

What an artist like Dryden (who supported the Restoration settlement and felt at home in the society it sanctioned) most needed was a cultural theory of an essentially conservative kind which was nevertheless sufficiently flexible and sufficiently realistic to permit fairly deep criticism of the established order from within its own basic social and cultural assumptions. This was supplied not by the more highfalutin claims of 'heroic' theory but by the more general and sober emphases and attitudes – the 'structures of feeling' – involved in neo-classicism.

What neo-classicism, in its broader sense, stressed was order, stability, acceptance of well-rationalized rules and a 'proper' sense of proportion. Hobbes's word 'discretion' tells us a lot about it. So does Professor Simon's summary of Dryden's view of the art of poetry as expressed in 1668 in his famous 'Essay of Dramatic Poesy': 'Poetry is an art; its object is to imitate nature. There are rules for obtaining this end, and these rules are known: they are those which Aristotle inferred from the practice of the ancients.'

Neo-classicism was an essentially conservative movement. It set great store on authority and decorum. And it permitted a writer like Dryden to adopt a view of English cultural development which saw the Court culture of the Restoration as in every important way superior to the condition of Elizabethan and Jacobean England. Behind neo-classical cultural theory is a massive confidence, shared by nearly all supporters of the settlements of 1660 and 1688, that the Restoration ushered in a society and a culture more rational and more civilized than the world of Shakespeare or Donne or Milton. And it is on the basis of this deep sense of cultural superiority that a writer like Dryden was able to accept the authority of the classics and the rules of what often seems to us, three hundred years later, a rather limited and élitist game. Yet if you approach Dryden's poetry too much obsessed by the limitations and reactionary implications of neo-classical cultural theory you will be missing something of key importance.

For 'neo-classicism' permitted not only the unrealistic bombast of the more rhetorical heroic tragedies, but also the satirical poise and rich ambiguities of the 'mock heroic'. *Absalom and Achitophel* is in one sense a deeply conservative work, politically and poetically. But (like the novels of Jane Austen at the other end of the 'Augustan' period) it is also a work which, through the veins and strata of irony which permeate it, questions and even undermines many of the very values it appears to exalt.

References

Burnley-Jones, T. and de Bear Nicol, B. (1976) *Neo-Classical Dramatic Criticism 1560–1770*, Cambridge University Press.

Dobrée, Bonamy (1929) *Restoration Tragedy*, Oxford University Press.

Hill, Christopher (1980, Revised edition) *The Century of Revolution*, Nelson. (*C of R*)

Hughes, Ann (ed) (1980) *Seventeenth-century England: A Changing Culture*, Vol 1 *Primary Sources*, Ward Lock. (Anthology)

Owens, W. R. (ed) (1980) *Seventeenth-century England: A Changing Culture*, Vol 2 *Modern Studies*, Ward Lock. (Reader)

Simon, Irène (1971) *Neo Classical Criticism 1660–1800*, Arnold.

Spingarn, J. E. (ed) (1968) *Critical Essays of the Seventeenth Century*, Oxford University Press.

Tillotson, Geoffrey (1964) *Augustan Poetic Diction*, Athlone Press.

'Absalom and Achitophel'

Contents

'Absalom and Achitophel'

1 Introduction

Absalom and Achitophel is a poem occasioned by a political crisis. There have been many other English poems about contemporary politics, but, generally speaking, they have not survived the situation which brought them into being. In reading this poem you must involve yourself imaginatively in the details of its historical context, and, at the same time, be prepared to stand back and consider its merits as a work of literature: whether you can, or should, separate these two activities is something to be thinking about.

You will find a modernized text of the poem in the Anthology, extract 134. Sections 3 and 4 of this course material will assist you in your first reading of the poem: the first 149 lines are recorded on Cassette 2 AC 206. You will later need to read article 26 'Dryden's Absalom' by Christopher Ricks in the Reader. It is a 'model' both by virtue of its ideas and perceptions, and in its presentation and marshalling of evidence to prove a case.

2 The Political Background

The Popish Plot, 1678–9

You will have already encountered the Popish Plot in *C of R* pp 168–7 and in the historical material by Professor J. R. Jones in Block 8 'From the Restoration to the Revolution of 1688'. My purpose is to remind you of a few details and to sketch in the implications.

In order to appreciate the mood of the time, look at *Figure 1*. Unlike a modern political cartoon, which usually has one scene with a punch line underneath, this tries to tell the whole story: a comic strip of the principal events of the Plot is presented, but it is dominated by a gallery of portraits. The Protestant martyr is at the top-centre, but notice that the King, larger than life-size, is also in a central position; although this is a piece of Opposition propaganda, the Opposition's case depended on convincing the people that the King's life was in danger – look at the little figures who surround him.

The British Museum catalogue reads:

> In the centre [is] a portrait of Sir E. B. Godfrey . . . inclosed in an oval frame, upon the border of which is written, '*Sr Edmund Burie Godfrey the Kingdom's Martyr* 1678;' and, in the background . . . '*the first Martyr on ye Account of this Damnable and Horrid Plot.*' The knight's expression is intensely lugubrious; round his neck is the handkerchief which was alleged to have been the instrument of his murder . . . The spandrils, filling the space between the exterior of this oval and the oblong within which it is inclosed, represent '*Fires and Massacres, Romish Mercies,* ' of '*London,* ' on one side, and, on the other, '*Southwark.*' At foot, '*Certainly this is the day they looked for. Jer. 1,*' and '*Whose Innocent Blood yet Cryes Vengeance, Vengeance!*' referring to Sir E. B. Godfrey.
>
> Beneath the oval is a whole-length portrait of Charles II., crowned, in royal robes, with sword and sceptre; behind him St. Paul's, a verse from Ps. xxxi. 17, with additions and illustrations, thus: '*While they took counsell against me they devised to take away my Life by Shot or Stab,*' as appears by the figures of '*Conyers,*' Anderton,

The Discoverers of the plot and Treasonable plotters.

Dr Oates. Mr Bedloe. Mr Prance. Mr Dugdale

Fires and Massacr

now or Never.

The Hellish Councell of the Whole Plot.

Lon don

KINGDOMS MARTYR. 1678

The first Martyr on y Accou and Ho

Fig: 2.

Mr Oates and Dr Tongs Information.

Fig: 3.

—Certainly this is t

Whose Innocen Vengeance

Fig: 1.

Psalm While counsell

by Poyson or Pistol

S.G.W

Justice Godfrey Drawn in is Strangled. up on

A Pretended Quarrel between Berry and Kelly.

Groves

Picker:

Fig: 4.

Fig: 5

Printed for Tho: Dawks the Designer of these Emblemes. 1679.

Figure 1 'England's Grand Memorial: The Unparallel'd Plot to destroy his Majesty; subvert the Protestant Religion; and Sir Edmund Burie Godfrey's Murder made Visible, Whereunto is added his Character.' British Museum 1064. (Reproduced by courtesy of the Trustees of the British Museum.)

and the '4 *Rufins*' who were said to have been employed in this manner against the king, '*by poyson*'—here is a figure of '*Sir G. W.,*' *i.e.* Sir George Wakeman, the queen's physician—'*Groves*' and '*Picker*' (Pickering) each armed with pistols, which are directed towards the king.

The print on each side of these portraits contains illustrations of the so-called plot, with, on the left side, portraits of '*The Discoverers of the Plot and Treasonable Plotters,*' four heads, of '*Dr. Oates,*' '*Mr. Bedloe,*' '*Mr. Prance,*' '*Mr. Dugdale.*' Beneath these, '*The Hellish Councell of the Whole Plot,*' five conspirators seated at table in a chamber, with the papal tiara before them, the Devil crying. '*Now or Never*' and '*Mr. Oates*' listening on the stairs. Next below is '*Mr. Oates and Dr. Tong's Information*' before Justice Godfrey. Next, '*Justice Godfrey Drawn in upon A Pretended Quarrel Between Berry and Kelly*' (who are pretending to fight with swords) '*is Strangled*' by four men, his wig and hat falling off in the struggle.

On the opposite side of the two portraits is, at top, '*Green twisting his neck about,*' '*Justice Godfrey exposed to the view of several persons,*' also '*Kelly, Green, Girald, Prance*' with '*Just: God: conveyed out*' in a sedan chair; the former two walking at the side of the others, who act as bearers. Next appears '*Justice Godfrey carried before Hills*' (on horseback), in company with '*Green, Girald, Kelly.*' Next—showing the body of Sir E. B. Godfrey as it was found, '*Gyrald Runneth Justice Godfrey's own sword thorow him.*' This was alleged to have been done in order to suggest suicide as the cause of death. By the side . . . is . . . '*Sir Edmund Burie Godfrey;*' anagram,—'*I find Murdered by Rouges.*' Below are two subjects: '*Murderers of Justice Godfrey,*' two men standing in a cart with ropes about their necks, and beneath the gibbet; and the drawing, hanging, and quartering of three men, '*The Heart and Bowels burnt of Traytors.*'

When you have read the poem, I hope you will turn back to this illustration; though it deals with earlier events, it seems to me to be a useful visual analogue to the structure of *Absalom and Achitophel* and to the way in which the poem's portraits stand out in the after-impression which we retain in our memory. This then is how political information, or propaganda, was conveyed at the time.

The Popish Plot was a fabrication, but it was believed to be true. The role of Titus Oates as the accuser may perhaps be compared to that of Senator McCarthy in the anti-communist 'hearings' in America after the Second World War. The situations are alike in that they show how national paranoia is generated; fear of subversion by a foreign power leads to an attack upon an unpopular minority within the country who are assumed to be enemy agents. The Thirty Years' War had exhausted the Protestant nations of Europe, and in the sixteen-seventies it became apparent that France was steadily increasing its influence and 'rolling back' its Northern frontier. Titus Oates (Corah in the poem) persuaded Parliament that he had evidence of a plot directed from France and involving prominent English Catholics: Charles II was to be assassinated and the Catholic Duke of York placed on the throne. Oates's story was believed because Sir Edmund Berry Godfrey, the magistrate to whom he had confided his story, was found murdered on 23 October 1678: and the discovery of the incriminating correspondence between Coleman, the Duke of York's secretary, and Louis XIV seemed to confirm the fact of a Catholic conspiracy. In the wave of hysteria which followed many innocent Catholics were executed.

Shaftesbury and the Exclusion Crisis, 1679–80

You will have noticed that the commemorative print (*Figure 1*) is dedicated to the Earl of Shaftesbury. As Achitophel he will be the villain of *Absalom and Achitophel,* but it is worth pointing out that his portrait in that poem has obliterated the ideals which he stood for. Believing that a Catholic ascendency in politics would lead to the absolutism of Louis XIV being imitated in England, he made use of the Plot to bring forward a series of Parliamentary Bills aimed at excluding James, Duke of York, from the succession. As Dryden points out in the poem, James was the legitimate heir, and Shaftesbury was proposing a theory of monarchy in which the people *elected* their ruler. Charles II had several illegitimate children, and one idea was that his son, the Protestant Duke of Monmouth, should succeed. He is of course the Absalom of the poem's title.

The events of 1681

With all these ingredients – religion once again a 'cause', the monarchy and the succession challenged – the Restoration settlement could have broken down. If things got out of hand, might there be another civil war? People were saying that 1641 had come again. Charles withdrew to Oxford (the Royalist capital in the sixteen-forties) and called Parliament to assemble there. Fortunately for Charles, he obtained secret offers of support from Louis XIV and was able to dissolve Parliament, so preventing the Exclusion Bill from becoming law. From then on the King took the initiative, and Shaftesbury was under attack: from 2 July 1681 he was imprisoned in the Tower of London.

The publication of 'Absalom and Achitophel', November 1681

It is said that the King suggested the idea of the poem to Dryden, but the comparison of Charles to David, and the identification of a false counsellor with the Biblical Achitophel had been made several times before. By now the rumours of a Popish Plot had been largely discredited. On the other hand, at this juncture Dryden seems to have been unwilling to publish a scurrilous verbal assault on Shaftesbury (which he was quite capable of, as in *The Medal: a Satire against Sedition*, published in 1682). What was required at this time was a balanced, ironic view of the political crisis, aimed at calming down a situation which might get out of control; the voice he adopts in the poem is that of a normal and reasonable person, with a historical overview. Events are seen in a humorous perspective: the Biblical parallels keep us at a distance. Dryden suggests that if only the parties would behave like gentlemen, national reconciliation would still be possible (see the Preface to the poem). *Absalom and Achitophel* was published anonymously, and ran to nine editions in two years.

3 An approach to the poem

Listen to lines 1–149. You will find these on Cassette 2, AC 206. *Please close the text for the first part of the discussion.*

(a) *Enjoying the poem.* I do hope – before we get down to sorting out who was who, and pointing to individual lines and important passages – that you are able to get pleasure from the *poem itself*. So much time has, inevitably, to be spend on *studying* a poem like this that it is easy to forget that it was once read without notes, and was, in its day, a best seller. I also believe that Dryden enjoyed writing it, and that he wrote the lines we have just been reading at speed. Try to free yourself, if you need to, from the nineteenth-century prejudice which assumes that poems about nature or some abstract joy or sorrow are automatically 'great', and that a poem which deals with contemporary politics is inevitably 'unpoetical' because of its subject matter. Listen to how the lines ring out – this is the fruit of twenty years' writing plays for performance, many of which were in the same heroic (i.e. couplet) verse as *Absalom and Achitophel*. (You will find an extract from one of Dryden's plays, *The Conquest of Granada*, in the Anthology, extract 133.) Notice the precision of the language, which was pointed out by the earliest 'reviewer', who said in the *Commendatory Verses* of 1682 that the unknown author

> The dialect, as well as sense, invents
> And with his poem a new speech presents.

Now try these exercises with the text still closed.
Fill in the rhymes to these couplets: the first one is done for you.

> Whether, inspired by some diviner lust,
> His father got him with a greater *gust;*
> Or that his conscious destiny made way,
> By manly beauty, to imperial _____ .
> Early in foreign fields he won renown,
> With kings and states allied to Israel's _____ :
> In peace the thoughts of war he could remove,
> And seemed as he were only born for _____ .
> Whate'er he did, was done with so much ease,
> In him alone 'twas natural to _____ :
> His motions all accompanied with grace;
> And Paradise was opened in his _____ .

If that was too easy, complete this section of the poem which you may not have read closely yet. The context is an argument that the legitimate successor may not be the best person to take the throne.

> Succession, for the general good designed,
> In its own wrong a nation cannot _____ ;
> If altering that the people can relieve,
> Better one suffer than a nation _____ .
> The Jews well know their power: ere Saul they chose,
> God was their King, and God they durst _____ .

Now check lines 19–30 and 413–18.

Whether you find this fascinating – or quite the opposite – you will find it an exercise which helps you to understand Dryden's craftmanship. In most cases the rhymes snap into place with an *inevitability* which may seem effortless, yet is the test of good writing. Notice how the *point* of each couplet is usually saved for the rhyming word. We will explore this in more detail in a moment.

(b) *The allusions to the Bible.* We must assume that the average seventeenth-century reader knew the Bible well. The heart of our story is in Samuel 2: 13–19, but provided you know that David was a great King of Israel and that Absalom was not only his rebellious but also his favourite and spoiled son, you can read on without looking it up. You could even consider whether Dryden wants us to remember the end of the story: *we* know that the historical fate of the Duke of Monmouth was remarkably close to that of Absalom, but Dryden didn't have this foreknowledge. The Biblical parallel is a warning: Absalom is still *redeemable* if he would only abandon his pretensions and detach himself from the false counsellor, Achitophel. The other biblical allusions are not precisely located to the time of King David: Dryden ranges all over the Old Testament, and even refers to the Temptation of Christ in the New Testament.

(c) *The seventeenth-century allusions.* Here, at least, you are probably better equipped than the average twentieth-century undergraduate reading English honours. You *know,* for example, all about Saul, Ishbosheth, and the restoration of King David (lines 57–60) and you don't need long footnotes explaining what happened from 1658–1660. Furthermore, you can see the retrospective compliment in calling Cromwell by the name of Saul, and Richard Cromwell is spiked with ridicule for all time in the comparison to Ishbosheth. (Don't be worried by having to look up Ishbosheth in a reference book: that's exactly what most people have to do when asked to identify Richard Cromwell – their utter forgetability is what they have in common.) If you enjoyed reading lines 57–60 and saw the point of the joke, then I can't see that the major historical references are going to cause you that much difficulty. Multi-disciplinary courses have their moments, and this is one of them.

4   Line by line commentary and discussion

Lines 1–10

EXERCISE

Notice how elegantly Monmouth's illegitimacy is explained without hurting the reputation of Charles II. What exactly does the word 'cursedly' do in line 4? How does David/Charles appear in lines 7–10?

DISCUSSION

'Cursedly' makes us feel that we are in the presence of a gentleman – 'Restoration rake' is perhaps too strong – who is somewhat irked by the restrictions of the marriage laws. The word also punctures the apparent seriousness of the opening. (This sudden let-down is a favourite technique of Dryden's.) The word also makes us ask from what point of view the poem is being written, and signals the irony and ambiguity which are a feature of this text.

David/Charles is seen as imitating the Creator: in 'scattering his Maker's image' he furthers the divine intention. So Charles II becomes by reflection, God-like. Or does he? It is simultaneously a compliment and a joke.

Lines 11–42

EXERCISE

What do you think is the purpose of this description? Who is at fault?

DISCUSSION

Absalom is perhaps 'too favourably' drawn ('Preface') if he is to become a dangerous rebel. The purpose surely is to present Absalom as a 'hero', but allusions such as that to Adam before his Fall (line 30) indicate that all is not well: there will be constant references back to *Paradise Lost* throughout the poem. It is Charles who is at fault for spoiling him.

Lines 43–135

This is a summary of the events which we went over on pp 23–7. You will need to go through these lines carefully, thinking about the tone and attitude of the narrator. It is a very neat summary of English history since 1650, but you know how much has been left out, and can see that it is propaganda for a point of view. But Dryden lays a false trail. The remarks about the Catholics (lines 107–21) are there to establish his credentials as a Protestant and to show that he is not one of the Crypto-Catholics about the Court.

EXERCISE

What is Dryden really frightened of?

'Absalom and Achitophel'

DISCUSSION

The people, their instability (line 45 following) and their tendency towards Republicanism. The words 'State' (line 66) and 'commonwealths' (line 84) should be given much more emotional significance than we would give them. They imply that governments made by man are, like the worship of the golden calf (line 66), against God, who alone has instituted monarchy in England. Contrast Milton's views on these points.

Lines 136–49

EXERCISE

What do you recognize here from your Milton studies?

DISCUSSION

Epic simile: Dryden's images of the stagnant pool working up into foam, and the fever in the blood, are combined into one frightening vision. The passage ends with references to *fiends* and rebels, reminiscent of the devils in Book I of *Paradise Lost*.

Figure 2   Nicolas Poussin The Adoration of the Golden Calf *c. 1635–7. (Reproduced by courtesy of the Trustees, The National Gallery, London.)*

Lines 150–219

The first section, down to say line 199, is usually printed in isolation in anthologies as 'the character of Achitophel'. In fact, it leads directly into narrative at the end, showing the character in action. The drawing of individuals in short and pithy paragraphs was a particular delight to writers and readers of the period. In verse, you can compare this passage to the description of the devils in Book I of *Paradise Lost:* Achitophel is Dryden's Satan.

EXERCISE

Remembering the exercise we began with, think about the difference in verse form between this and *Paradise Lost*. How does Dryden use the couplet here? What does rhyme give him which Milton hasn't got? *Read the passage again slowly before answering.*

DISCUSSION

Balance and wit. It's epigrammatic, and therefore memorable. The mere giving of information and simple narrative are not the best use of rhyming couplets, because they can lead to unnecessary padding. Here, on the other hand, the enclosure of each couplet contains *one* striking idea:

> Great wits are sure to madness near allied,
> And thin partitions do their bounds divide;

or *several* points are balanced against each other:

> In friendship false, implacable in hate;
> Resolved to ruin or to rule the State.

Notice here that it could have been 'rule' and 'ruin', ignoring metrical considerations. This order implies that his rule will be just as ruinous.

This witty reversal is there in the rhyme as well. The natural ending to line 151 is 'A name to all succeeding ages bless'd'. The first couplet has become over-familiar, but the word 'cursed' must have seemed both unexpectedly fresh and yet strikingly true. The rhyme punches the point home.

There are many examples of this unexpectedness. Look at lines 206–7, where the fearless judge of lines 187–91 is reduced to a tactician who '*skulked* behind the laws.' In the next couplet quite common words 'takes' and 'finds' are balanced against the seemingly innocuous 'makes' – until we think what is being said.

EXERCISE

What, as we might say today, seems to be Achitophel's problem? And why is he a threat?

DISCUSSION

There's plenty to say here, and a short answer is bound to be too simple. All I can do is to start you off. Look back to line 42 'And David, undisturbed, in Sion reigned . . .'. Achitophel is unable to accommodate himself to the peace of Charles's 'heavenly kingdom'. He is the victim of a disease of hyperactivity, which will not let his body rest. In fact, lines 156–8 refer to Shaftesbury's illness. John Locke, who was his doctor, directed a surgeon to drain a cyst on the liver by means of a silver tap: so here Achitophel's soul, his vital spirits, overflow ('o'er-inform') his body ('the tenement of clay'). His restlessness, his changing sides – from Royalist to Cromwellian, from Charles's Minister to being the leader of the Opposition – represents a threat to the stability of the state. It's admitted that he is clever ('Great wits') but God preserve us from intelligent politicians . . .

Now make your own notes about this character, concentrating on the points made in each couplet.

Figure 3   Anthony Ashley-Cooper, Earl of Shaftesbury (1621–83) after John Greenhill. (Reproduced by courtesy of the Trustees, National Portrait Gallery, London.)

Lines 220–490
You may read these lines rapidly, thinking mainly of the story.

EXERCISE

How would you entitle this section of the poem? Does anything remind you of Milton?

DISCUSSION

The Temptation of Absalom. Compare, as you must, the various temptation scenes in Milton. Besides the temptation of Eve by Satan, some of you may know that *Paradise Regained* is about the Temptation of Christ in the wilderness. There is an echo of Milton's style in line 373 which I want to discuss later.

Lines 471–6 are not Miltonic, but typically 'Restoration' in their sexual imagery. Historically, it's a reference back to Cornet Joyce and the man-

32

oeuverings of the various parties in the late sixteen-forties 'to possess the prince'. As contemporary readers would be well aware, taking 'possession of the Prince' had been made treasonable by the Act to Preserve the Person and Government of the King (1661), so that Achitophel's advice culminates (like Satan's) in a proposal to commit a capital offence.

Lines 491–681

Now read lines 491–681, noticing particularly the characters of Zimri and Corah. The third main section of the poem is the list of conspirators. First of all we are given a general view of the various interests and factions: after listing the nobility and the commercial classes, we come to the London mob (line 513), the Dissenting ministers (lines 519–28) and the remains of the radical sects 'A numerous host of dreaming saints succeed' (lines 529–32). Finally, the mob becomes monstrous 'sprouting heads' (line 542).

Lines 543–68 contain the character of Zimri, which is also frequently authologized, and even quoted in Parliament (1978).

EXERCISE

Zimri is not so dangerous as Achitophel, though he shares the vice of restlessness. Why not?

Figure 4   'Titus Oates. Anagramma Testis Ovat'. Portrait from the life at the height of his fame by R. White, 1679. British Museum 1073. (Reproduced by courtesy of the Trustees of the British Museum.)

Figure 5   'Testis Ovat'. Oates in the pillory, 1685. British Museum 1135. (Reproduced by courtesy of the Trustees of the British Museum.)

DISCUSSION

He is the dilettante, who has more money than sense (line 559): in the end nobody takes him seriously. You will need to work at the language and variety of the couplets as we did for Achitophel. Dryden thought that this character was 'worth the whole poem'. Note that in real life there was a violent personal antagonism between Dryden and the Duke of Buckingham. But he doesn't take the opportunity to write scurrilously, and so you wouldn't know this from the character of Zimri. At a later stage you could consider whether this character exemplifies Dryden's aim in satire.

The list of conspirators continues (lines 569–629) until we reach the final place of honour.

EXERCISE

In dealing with Corah (Titus Oates) lines 630–81 the attitude of the narrator is quite different. How would you describe it?

DISCUSSION

After a short burst of wit to keep us in trim – 'thou shalt from oblivion *pass*' (line 632) – implying that the most famous 'witness' of the Popish Plot had already been forgotten, Dryden stands back in apparent wonder at this phenomenon, this 'comet', and tells us his story as if it was 'a log-cabin to White House' legend, or Samuel Smiles' biography of a great entrepreneur: 'What though his birth were base' (line 636). The trouble is that nothing is quite as it should be. Comets (line 636) must fall, prodigies (line 638) aren't necessarily great and could be monstrous, and in lines 642–3 Stephen was a good man attacked by bad witnesses. In line 645 'God Almighty's gentlemen' can hardly be taken straight – in fact 'God Almighty' was Oates's favourite expletive – and from line 646 the signs of Oates's character become more and more ambiguous. In line 647 the negatives are wrong. In lines 648–9 he looks like a red-face clown, though it's true that Moses's face did shine on Sinai and so we are temporarily re-assured. But what about 'miraculously' (line 650), which is obviously ironic, as is (line 655) 'where the witness failed, the prophet spoke . . .'. Finally, as is often Dryden's method, the whole edifice collapses into bathos with the double-meaning of 'the Lord knows where', and the allusion to Oates's so-called doctorate from the University of Salamanca. In the last lines (lines 664 following) Dryden rushes in to defend his victim and even offers to take Oates's place; leading to further revelation of the methods his victim employed.

Lines 682–932

Now read lines 682–810 for the story.

The conspiracy gathers momentum, as Absalom is launched on a 'vote-catching' tour of the country (lines 682–810). He has now become a Tempter himself, and 'glides' serpent-like into the people's hearts. He adopts the persuasive skills he has learnt from Achitophel (lines 698–722) and begins a progress through the West Country (lines 729–50). At this point Dryden stands back and addresses the gentle reader – 'What shall we think?' (line 759). He assumes that we will agree with the arguments of the political conservative: we must leave the British constitution alone . . . 'innovation is the blow of fate' (lines 795–810).

Now read lines 811–932. Here we are given the portraits of the King's friends, a catalogue of David's party. Though meant to counterbalance the rebels, inevitably the good characters do not inspire Dryden to use his full spirit and energy; in any case they are not open to the kind of witticisms and ridicule which the rebels deserve.

Lines 933–1031

Now read from line 933 to the end of the poem.

EXERCISE

What is the King's speech about? Sort out the hopes and wishes from the decrees. If you have time, look up God's speech from the throne of heaven in Book III of *Paradise Lost*.

DISCUSSION

The speech is modelled upon that of Milton's all-seeing and fore-knowing God. It also refers to Charles's address to the nation in March 1681. For a long time there had been some doubt as to Charles's intentions, and the first part shows him 'winding himself up' to action (lines 943–50) and realizing his own danger: he will stand by James because the throne itself is threatened (lines 975–990). Having at last formed a resolution – this is the real theme of the speech – lines 1000–5 show him still wavering. But 1010–15 is forceful and direct – '"By their own arts"' and '"Against themselves their witnesses will swear"' – the Irish witnesses who were supposed to swear to the truth of an Irish Plot will change sides and appear *against* Shaftesbury at his trial. It is Shaftesbury who will bleed (line 1011) and the Whigs will end up fighting among themselves (line 1016). This prophecy did not lose its point even when the Grand Jury returned an ignoramus verdict on 24 November, as Charles had recovered control of the situation.

The final lines of the poem announce the return of the Golden Age, a favourite theme of Dryden's.

Conclusion

This introductory commentary was intended to help you with your first reading of the poem. When you feel ready for a more advanced discussion please turn to article 26 by Christopher Ricks in the Reader, which fills out this commentary.

5   What kind of a poem?

Is it satire?

Absalom and Achitophel is usually described as a 'satire' in literary histories. Before embarking on a discussion of this please look at another poem in the Anthology 'An Expostulation with Inigo Jones' by Ben Jonson (extract 17). This is an example of a 'flyting' or an attack upon an individual. It also contains a defence of the rights of a dramatist as opposed to a mere scene-painter ('O shows . .' line 39 to 'masque' line 50).

EXERCISE

How does Dryden's poem resemble or differ from this example?

DISCUSSION

Two points of difference strike me immediately. Firstly, the personal and abusive element which most people associate with satire is only present in descriptions of the 'characters' which take up about one-fifth of Dryden's poem: and in these, according to his own 'Preface', Dryden is deliberately muting his attack. Dryden is also on record, in *A Discourse Concerning the Original and Progress of Satire*, as saying that any fool can attack a personality with scurrilous obscenities – the real art is to be so subtle that one can remove the head from the body without the victim being aware. (You will find the relevant passage on Cassette 3, AC 207. The passage is reprinted in Cassette Notes 3.) The victims in his poem are so memorable that we allow them to colour our view of the whole poem.

Secondly, there is a political element in Dryden's poem. Most political satire is written by the opposition in any age; Dryden is unusual in that if this is satire it is on behalf of the Government of the day, and on behalf of the established order. This would seem to be an exceedingly difficult position from which to write an all-embracing 'satire'.

Is it panegyric?

This is not a common form in English, and might be described as a flattering poem about a great man. Look at extract 132 from *Astraea Redux* in the Anthology, commemorating Charles's restoration in 1660, which could be described as a panegyric. Notice the description of Dover strand (compare *Absalom and Achitophel*, lines 270–2), and the Virgilian idea of a new 'series' of Time, which Dryden used again at the end of *Absalom and Achitophel*. It seems to me that a good deal of *Absalom and Achitophel* is written in the style of a panegyric (look for example at lines 317ff), and as such it could be described as a celebration of the God-King's imminent victory over his enemies.

Is it a minor epic?

Or in seventeenth-century terms, is it 'an heroic poem'? It was always Dryden's intention to compose an epic poem about King Arthur (remember that Milton had the same idea), but it was put off and put off as the demands of day-to-day work increased. Dryden had to write plays for a living. He firmly believed that 'An heroic poem . . . is undoubtedly the greatest work which the soul of man is capable to perform.' See further extract 135 in the Anthology, 'Tragedy and the Epic'.

Is it mock-heroic?

'Mock-heroic' should perhaps be explained. Unlike mock-turtle, it is not a substitute for the heroic, but a poem which in some sense mocks the heroic original. The reader must be *conscious* of the original – whether as a general notion or form, or by reference to a specific work. Because it *depends* on the original it often seems to borrow some of its dignity. As a critical term it is best applied to a work like Pope's *Rape of the Lock*, which burlesques the conventions of epic.

EXERCISE

Thinking back over your work on both poems, what points of comparison have you noticed between 'Paradise Lost' and 'Absalom and Achitophel'?

DISCUSSION

You may have noticed that both the title pages of *Paradise Lost* and *Absalom and Achitophel* are sub-titled 'A Poem'. I take this to be deliberate, and that a heroic poem is intended in each case. Without going over all the detailed points raised in the Commentary, though all of them could be used to make the case, the three major areas of comparison are the story, the style, and the structure. Both poems contain at their centre a story of temptation and fall: Absalom = Adam, Achitophel = Satan, and Charles/David = God. (There are two references in the 'Preface' to *Absalom and Achitophel* which are relevant. They are on p 300 and p 301 where Dryden says 'it is no more a wonder that [Absalom] withstood not the temptations of Achitophel, than it was for Adam not to have resisted the two devils, the serpent and the woman' and 'God is infinitely merciful; and his viceregent [Charles II] is only not so, because he is not infinite.') Dryden makes a deliberate echo of the style of *Paradise Lost* at one point, which contrasts with the usual flow of his syntax: 'Him staggering so when hell's dire agent found . . .' (line 373). This must be intentional, and can only be described as mock-heroic. Finally look at the long argumentative speeches in both poems and their arrangement; there are five in *Absalom and Achitophel* and they are carefully spaced out within the poem, culminating in the speech from the throne.

More might be said, but I think it should be clear that Dryden is consciously competing with Milton, whom he greatly admired. He is alleged to have said, after reading *Paradise Lost* 'This man cuts us all out and the ancients too'. This is a nice compliment, but it comes from a man who is in the race himself. The relationship between the two poems may in fact be too close, and the resulting work too complex to be easily classifiable. The author of the *Commendatory Verses* of 1682 may have the last word. In praising the anonymous writer of *Absalom and Achitophel* he said it was:

> As if a Milton from the dead arose
> Filed off the rust and the right party chose . . .

6 Dryden's achievement

Absalom and Achitophel seemed to us an appropriate poem to study at this stage in the course. It both sums up and sends up political and religious concerns of the whole century. It made people see that one could laugh at all kinds of things which in the earlier part of the century would have been considered too sacred, or so contentious that they led to civil war. From now on neither the person of the monarch nor the Bible is sacred, and political disputes about these institutions are a waste of energy besides being distinctly old-fashioned and ungentlemanly. One thinks of Swift and the quarrels of the Lilliputians over high and low heels or the best way to open an egg.

The first two hundred lines of *Absalom and Achitophel* are one of the longest *sustained* passages of good writing in our literature. Speaking more generally, and you will need to read more widely in Dryden's works to substantiate this, Dryden felt that he had devoted his life to writing clearly and helping others towards this simple ideal. In a letter written at the end of his life he described himself as 'a man who has done my best to improve the language and especially the poetry.'

In his poetry he laid the groundwork for generations of later writers to build upon: besides the obvious point that Pope and most other Augustan poets used and developed the heroic couplet, remember that Keats studied Dryden while working on 'Lamia' and the Odes, and that Hopkins called him 'the most masculine of our poets: his style and rhythms lay the strongest stress of all our literature on the naked thew and sinew of the English language.' It seems best, however, to leave Dr Johnson with the last word:

> Of Dryden's works it was said by Pope that 'he could select from them better specimens of every mode of poetry than any other English writer could supply.' Perhaps no nation ever produced a writer that enriched his language with such variety of models. To him we owe the improvement, perhaps the completion of our metre, the refinement of our language, and much of the correctness of our sentiments. By him we were taught 'sapere et fari', to think naturally and express forcibly. Though Davies has reasoned in rhyme before him, it may be perhaps maintained that he was the first who joined

argument with poetry. He showed us the true bounds of a translator's liberty. What was said of Rome, adorned by Augustus, may be applied by an easy metaphor to English poetry embellished by Dryden, 'lateritiam invenit, marmoream reliquit', he found it brick, and he left it marble.

(*Life of Dryden*)

Recommended books

Editions

The Poems of John Dryden, 4 vols (ed James Kinsley) (1958) Oxford University Press.
Poems and Fables of John Dryden, (1962) Oxford Standard Authors, Oxford University Press. A shortened version of the above.

Selections

Selected Poems: John Dryden (ed Roger Sharrock) (1963) Heinemann.
Dryden: Absalom and Achitophel and Other Poems, (ed Philip Roberts) (1973) Collins.

Faber and Methuen also publish selections.

Criticism

van Doren, Mark (1920) *The Poetry of John Dryden* (later editions called *John Dryden: A Study of his Poetry*).
Jack, Ian (1952) *Augustan Satire 1660–1750*, Oxford University Press.
Miner, Earl (1967) *Dryden's Poetry*, Indiana University Press.

Historical background

Haley, K. H. D. (1968) *The First Earl of Shaftesbury*, Oxford University Press.
Kenyon, J. P. (1972) *The Popish Plot*, Heinemann.

A Restoration Comedy: 'The Man of Mode'

Contents

A Restoration Comedy: 'The Man of Mode'

Introduction

We are coming to the end of a very full course and it is only realistic to recognize that your time and energy may now be running out. Accordingly I have designed this material so that it can be studied in two ways: a thin but I hope not misleading survey of the material based on a study of the play's first act which will help round out your study of the post-Restoration period, and a more seaching enquiry which you should follow if you wish to write about this play in an assignment or in the final exam. Fortunately Etherege's own skilful construction is helpful here because the first scene carefully introduces nearly all of the vital aspects of the play.

Begin by revising those sections of Margot Heinemann's commentary on *Women Beware Women* in Block 2 which describe the state of the theatre in the early decades of the seventeenth century (pp 47–56).

Next, read the first section (pp 11–28) of the 'Introduction' to your edition of *The Man of Mode* in *Three Restoration Comedies* ed. Gamini Salgado (Penguin Books, 1968). This is important because it briefly describes what happened to the theatres during the Civil War, and what ways the re-opened theatres of the Restoration were like and unlike the theatres of the earlier period.

Now, before you read the play, you may find the following advice useful. The plot of this and many other comedies of the period is not easy to follow. Salgado quotes the famous Edwardian director Harley Granville Barker: 'How could an audience both be clever enough to understand the story and stupid enough to be interested by it when they did?' The most likely answer is that the original audiences were clever enough to see that the plot does not matter. It is much more important to be aware that this play (and many other comedies of the period) is *about people who themselves like plotting*. (So of course, in a darker vein, was *Women Beware Women*.) It is not important to know exactly who has arranged – say – that Mrs Loveit should meet Sir Fopling and why. But it is important to realize that Mrs Loveit, Dorimant and Belinda (indeed most of the major characters) are constantly trying to manipulate other people for their own advantage. Paradoxically the people on the stage often seem to be directing fragmentary plays themselves. They arrange tableaux that can be seen and interpreted like a scene on the stage: Mrs Loveit has to be seen to be encouraging Sir Fopling. They stage-manage their exits and entrances. When Dorimant's plot is turned against him he comments ironically 'Damn her! I am jealous of a counter-plot' (p 100). Above all the actors must present characters who are themselves constantly disguising their feelings, affecting fashionable behaviour and imitating attitudes not their own: in another word, acting. So here the stage which traditionally in Hamlet's words, holds 'a mirror up to nature' reflects a world where people like to behave as if they were on a stage.

The play has two plots, and Harriet features in both. In the sub-plot (less important because it does not include Dorimant) Young Bellair wants to marry Emilia, but will be disinherited if he does not conform to his father's wishes and marry Harriet – who is very rich. In the main plot Harriet is determined to attract the famous rake Dorimant who at first has no intention of marrying anyone despite his estate's need for an heiress's fortune. (Salgado's summary at the top of p 31 is not an accurate description of the sub-plot where neither Harriet, Emilia nor Young Bellair disagrees about who wants whom.)

1   The first scene: an introduction to some of the major themes of the play

Whether or not you plan to go on to the work on the rest of the play which follows, you should read Act 1 scene i now, and consult the text when necessary. I have given page numbers to the Penguin edition.

Before the curtain rises a Prologue is addressed to the audience which is remarkable for its insulting attitude towards the audience and its ironic insistence that foreign – and especially French – follies are no better than the native kind.

The opening scene shows us the kind of characters the play is about, their world and their values and the problems that we expect will be resolved before the final curtain.

Dorimant's first lines strike a note which will characterize the whole play: kind words to a mistress he is tired of are like taxes which the citizen is expected to pay though he never does it gladly. He assumes his cynical attitude to women will be generally accepted, and that the payment of taxes which at the beginning of our period of study was no laughing matter has become just that.

The brief dialogue with his valet Handy shows that although Dorimant may conduct his amours more decorously than his servants there is no real difference between them. This is confirmed twice: first by Foggy Nan the orange-woman, then by Swearing Tom the shoemaker. Both confirm that Dorimant's superior manners are no more than a gloss on the common appetite. Foggy Nan supplies him with fruit and a good tip about a likely woman quite indiscriminately; and in both commodities she is pleased to supply only the best. (Throughout the play fruit symbolizes sexual appetite as if a parody of the Fall were being constantly re-enacted.) But social upheavals seem to have affected even the bawdy trade and Foggy Nan finds it hard to get her money now that gentlemen like Dorimant undertake their own procuring.

Another aspect of social mobility is satirically presented in Swearing Tom (one of a long tradition of radical shoemakers) who in his commonest vices ironically sees himself aping the gentry:

> 'Zbud, there's never a man i'the town lives more like a gentleman with his wife than I do. I never mind her motions, she never inquires into mine; we speak to one another civilly, hate one another heartily, and because 'tis vulgar to lie and soak together, we have each of us our several settle-bed. (p 57)

The three dialogues with Handy, Foggy Nan and Swearing Tom all ironically invert traditional moral criteria: 'Whoring and swearing are vices too genteel for a shoemaker' says Medley (p 56), Dorimant's rather colourless side-kick. But the apparent knockabout egalitarianism of all this is only a thin skin over vast social distinctions: Dorimant makes no bones about reminding Handy and Foggy Nan of the power of his purse (the next servant who gets the pox 'shall rot for an example' because Dorimant will not pay a surgeon) and if the shoemaker goes too far he will 'stand i' the pillory': yet all three (Dorimant is dressing as this scene proceeds) are essential to the maintenance of the fashionable gentleman. The social difference between them gives Foggy Nan a perspective which none of the fine ladies in the play is quite able to achieve: 'Lord, would the ladies had heard you talk of 'em as I have done!' (p 50). Lady Woodvill, Harriet's mother, is (we learn) 'a great admirer of the forms and civilities of the last age'. In the course of the play she is generally made fun of because her blinkered insistence that the old ways were best is one of the forces that turns her daughter towards Dorimant and not against him as she intended. But she does serve as a reminder that times have indeed changed and two of the changes that her old-fashioned attitudes highlight are of special interest to us: the general light use of religious language and the altered standing of women. The second of these points will be discussed later.

Lady Woodvill thinks Dorimant is an 'arrant devil' (p 52) and later she says 'He has a tongue . . . would tempt the angels to a second fall' (p 95). But imputations such as these, made with dreadful seriousness by Lady Woodvill, are accepted with a light heart by Dorimant and his cronies. I have already suggested that the offering and taking of the peach might be acted as a parody of the Fall. Quite unambiguous however is the bandying about of terms which in the previous generation would have been the subjects of the most serious debate. Medley greets Dorimant as 'my life, my joy, *my darling-sin*' (p 51). Foggy Nan uses 'heathen' as a simple term of abuse (p 51) and takes her leave with the words 'Now do you long to be *tempting* this pretty creature' (p 54). Both Dorimant and Medley use the devil's name merely as a form of emphasis. There is nothing new in this of course but as the play develops we become more and more aware that the names of God and the devil and religious concepts like sin and temptation are constantly used in a frivolous and secular context but are never taken seriously. Now, obviously serious religious debate is unlikely in any comedy but as the play progresses we increasingly feel that it imitates and is addressed to a part of society which is glad that the heat has (temporarily at least) gone out of religious controversies. (See *C of R* Chapter 15, the first two sections.) The shoemaker has no religious beliefs ('The orange-woman says your neighbours take notice what a heathen you are, and design to inform the bishop and have you burned for an atheist' p 56) and the clergy are only useful for performing weddings. Look at the exchange between Medley and Young Bellair on p 58 where both relish the profane use of religious language. (Look also at Salgado's 'Introduction' pp 11–12, 25–6, 31–2.)

The first description of Harriet (pp 52–3) establishes not just her beauty and great wealth (without which she wouldn't stand a chance) but her 'wit', 'malice' and wildness. Harriet was the liveliest and most interesting heroine of Restoration comedies up to this date. She had to be, of course, if the match with Dorimant (himself the cleverest and most cynical of heroes) was going to work in any sense. 'Malice' can only be a commendable quality in a society quite candid about its own competitiveness. And that piquant combination of wildness and demure looks is exactly what a man like Dorimant wants: a certified virgin with the bedroom propensities of a practised courtesan. She needs exceptional qualities, looks and wealth if she is to get by in a society where women are treated so contemptuously. When old Bellair complains that Emilia, who is in love with his son but must put up with being teased and fondled by the father, is 'too serious', Lady Townley comments drily 'The fault is very excusable in a young woman' (p 65). And Lady Woodvill comments: 'Well, this is not the women's age, let 'em think what they will. Lewdness is the business now, love was the business in my time' (p 103). Perhaps this is only something that the mothers of young women have said in every generation. But she is right up to a point: the age which this comedy represents is not 'the women's age'. The status of women had actually declined (see Radio programmes 1 and 12), though the female characters in these plays cheated by men do not think so, nor have most of the critics and producers who have studied them since. But Etherege understood the situation better. It is significant that after a long eclipse when plays such as this were considered too lewd to be staged they began to return to the repertoire in substantial numbers in the nineteen-fifties and there was quite a glut of Restoration comedy in the early nineteen-sixties. These revivals happened at a time of rather premature rejoicing over the so-called new sexual freedom of women which was in that respect comparable to the Restoration period itself.

At the beginning of our period it was not uncommon for a woman to share in the family's business. But it is quite clear that no fashionable lady in

The Man of Mode would wish to be associated with anything so demeaning –
a change that we saw beginning in *Women Beware Women*, where Bianca has
been reared to be no more than a luxury and an ornament for the man who
will gain, with her, possession of her wealth. In the fine ladies of the comedies that follow the Restoration we can see that far from being honoured for
their usefulness, these women are valued as status symbols, indices of wealth
that enables them to lead a totally idle life. In the town, within the relatively
narrow circle of those who could afford to do nothing, the fashionable round
of artificial activities would pass the time away. The countryside was
anathema to these people, though it was the country that was the source of
their wealth, because they could find nothing to do there. 'I know all beyond
High-Park's a desart to you' says Harriet to Dorimant (p 136).

Salgado quotes from *Paradise Lost* Book IV on p 26 of the 'Introduction'.
It is clear that Milton valued Eve far more highly than the men in this play
value her daughters. It is important to distinguish between Dorimant's
evaluation and Etherege's. For although it is clear that Dorimant is seen as
the pattern of a fashionable gentleman and wit, the morality of the attitudes
he displays with such aplomb do not go unquestioned – a point our television dramatization emphasizes (Television programme 14). The way in
which Etherege orders his material in the first act makes this plain. Dorimant
is dressing for business, and his business is women. In the course of this scene
some kind of sexual relationship is postulated – past, present, future or
putative – between Dorimant and *every* young woman in the play and one
who never appears but suggests innumerable others like herself: that is,
Molly who wants 'a guynie to see the operies' (p 63).

The scene begins with Mrs Loveit, to whom attention is now a tax
(p 49). When Dorimant hears that Harriet is not only beautiful and 'vastly
rich' (p 52) but wants to know him, he comments drily: 'Flesh and blood
cannot hear this and not long to know her' (p 53). Dorimant has pretended
that 'business' has kept him away from Mrs Loveit, but as Medley knows,
'This business . . . has been with a vizard at the playhouse . . .' (p 54): that is,
Belinda. Comic exaggeration does not altogether conceal a sadistic streak in
Dorimant:

> Next to the coming to a good understanding with a new mistress, I
> love a quarrel with an old one. But the devil's in't; there has been
> such a calm in my affairs of late, I have not had the pleasure of
> making a woman so much as break her fan, to be sullen, or forswear
> herself these three days. (p 55)

Medley offers to interfere, but Belinda has already offered to provoke her
predecessor to a quarrel. Throughout the play the uneasy relationship that
competitiveness forces on these two women is carefully studied. Etherege
sees as clearly as Middleton that women will betray each other to men
because men call the tune. I have called the fuller discussion of this aspect of
the play 'Ladies beware Ladies' to remind you of the comparisons and contrasts that can be made with the earlier play.

Even Emilia, in love with Young Bellair, is almost automatically
included in Dorimant's survey. Although at present she is a 'discreet maid' (p
61) Dorimant's estimation is that once married she will make no difficulty
about cuckolding her husband. It is in his own future interests that he has
urged Young Bellair to marry her, not because he is an admirer of mat-
rimony. He does not express any such cynicism about the conduct of Harriet, his own intended wife – of course.

Marriage with anyone is never considered for either Mrs Loveit or
Belinda. The status of both is very vague. They are acceptable in fashionable
society and Belinda's secret relationship with Dorimant is never disclosed –
an ominous little time-bomb surely, deliberately placed by Etherege to
undermine the conventional happy ending. There is no sign of a Mr Loveit –
Restoration comedies are full of such ambiguous ladies. One thing is very
clear: a fashionable man is not expected to be chaste; a fashionable woman

must be chaste before marriage and though she is expected to be adulterous after marriage she will be despised for it.

Yet beyond maintaining his perfectly presented self, Dorimant needs to do little to keep himself constantly supplied with compliant women. They come to him. Mrs Loveit cannot give him up despite endless proof of how he despises her. Belinda willingly clears the way to her own only half-happy seduction. Harriet loses most of the little power she has because from the beginning Dorimant knows she is interested in him. Dorimant is the well-dressed embodiment of a very primitive male fantasy. The final touch in Etherege's powerfully satirical analysis of the sexual behaviour of his contemporaries is that during this scene in which they are all effectively disposed of, none of the women actually appear: their absence shows how little they are valued for themselves. Though they all later seem to be so actively conniving it is not for their own real advancement. Save for the actual bedding (and of course the money that an heiress will bring to marriage) men can get on very nicely without women, who have been gulled into doing much of the men's work in the matter of their own seduction for them. It is not just the relative proprieties of the late seventeenth century which prevented more overt sexual behaviour on stage. The society which plays like this present seems to think more of talking about sex than about sex itself. Dorimant is as much interested in the power he has over women as the pleasure he takes in bed. After a hasty seduction Belinda is bundled out with little more ceremony than the soiled linen (p 115).

The whole play insistently draws our attention to dress, affectations and manners and the way outward behaviour presents or disguises the inner self. A ridiculously over-dressed and affected character like Sir Fopling Flutter appears in many plays of this period, but this one is remarkable because Dorimant himself is also so conscious of his appearance: 'I love to be well dressed, sir, and think it no scandal to my understanding' (p 59). When Young Bellair sums up Sir Fopling (p 60) he is not far from describing Dorimant. Indeed, though Salgado assumes (as the alternative titles of the play at first appear to suggest) that the man of mode *is* Sir Fopling Flutter, it becomes increasingly likely as our knowledge of the play deepens that Dorimant must also be thought of as a man of mode whom we should measure by comparison with Sir Fopling. Besides his pleasure in dress he is an epicure of wit and kind of dandy in his sexual behaviour. You will find this point discussed in Salgado's 'Introduction' pp 32–3.

Sir Fopling self-consciously studies his own attitudes: 'His head stands for the most part on one side, and his looks are more languishing than a lady's when she lolls at stretch in her coach or leans her head carelessly against the side of box i' the playhouse' (p 59). All the major characters in this play are aware of the characteristic behaviour and mannerisms of others. One of the first things we learn about Harriet is that she *imitates* Dorimant: 'acted with head and with her body so like you . . .' (p 51). Later, she and Young Bellair will imitate being in love with one another so convincingly that their parents will be persuaded their plans are going smoothly. This pervasive habit of imitation and the general belief that well-bred people do not reveal their feelings may make us wonder whether these people are capable of genuine feeling at all. Even the shoemaker and his wife ape the gentry when they get drunk together. It is because he is the ridiculous epitome of all such studied behaviour that Sir Fopling has so prominent a place in the play. He only carries to excess those arts that are essential to the proper self-esteem of all these sophisticated people.

2   The treatment and development of the play's themes

As I said earlier, you need read no further if you only have time to attempt a general survey of post-Restoration culture. But if you wish to write on any topic that requires detailed reference to the literature of this period (either in an assignment or in the examination) you should work carefully through this final section on *The Man of Mode*. Before starting on this however, read the rest of the play.

The short sections that follow take up themes that have been introduced in the discussion of the first scene of the play and explore their development in the later scenes. Each begins with references to scenes or dialogues of special relevance to that theme and you should read them carefully and then turn to the questions and exercises in the study material. What I have written on the first scene is fairly self-contained. But the material in these short sections deliberately does not form a piece of continuous exposition. Though I offer some guidance the work there is open-ended, and left for you to complete.

Imitation, mimicry and manners

This is the longest section and it includes discussion of quite a large proportion of the play. When you have completed it you will see that the work in the three much shorter sections which follow depends upon it. Read each scene as it is listed below and answer the questions which follow. They are mostly quite straightforward and are designed to help you assemble a useful body of notes. My response to some (but not the most straightforward) of the questions follows each subsection.

EXERCISE

(a)   *The dialogue between Emilia and Medley on p 68*
What is Medley's attitude to French (and other foreign) ideas about correct behaviour?

Do you think any of the characters in the play might have studied *The Art of Affectation* already? (One has certainly studied something similar, but there are others who display various degrees of affectation.)

(b)   *Dorimant's words to Belinda and Mrs Loveit on p 74*
What kind of person does Dorimant say he will imitate in the speech beginning 'It must be so', and why would such behaviour threaten Belinda?

Cynically, Dorimant ascribes his callous treatment of Mrs Loveit to honesty, 'good nature and good manners' (p 74). Is his honesty at this point commendable? What point do you think Etherege wants to make about good manners?

(c)   *The whole of Act III scene i*
Why is Harriet angry?
How did she persuade her mother to bring her to London?
Why does Young Bellair expect Harriet to be angry?
Why is Harriet able to deceive 'their gravities' – the parents – so well? What phrase does she use to describe her pretence?

(d)   *Sir Fopling's visit to Lady Townley's house pp 87–91*
How do the others make fun of Sir Fopling?

Compare the frequent French words and phrases with the instructions cited in *The Art of Affectation* on p 68. What is the point of this anti-French satire? (See 'The French Example', pp 18–20 above and the Prologue to *The Man of Mode*.)

Why do the rest despise Sir Fopling so thoroughly?

(Notice that at the end of this scene the 'old' man referred to is Old Bellair. Lady Townley mimics his absurd teasing and Emilia responds accordingly.)

(e)   *The dialogue between Harriet and Young Bellair at the bottom of p 92 up to Dorimant's entrance on p 93*
Is Harriet merely pretending to think Dorimant affected? Or is there some truth in what she says? (See p 44.)

(f) *The dialogue between Harriet and Dorimant pp 93–5*

Why does Harriet say that Dorimant shall not know that her emotions have changed as much as her appearance?

Why do they deliberately use *double entendres* which they can both understand?

Why does Harriet suddenly decide to leave?

Why does the exchange end with them both imitating one another?

(g) *The exchanges between Mrs Loveit and Sir Fopling and Belinda, Dorimant and Medley on pp 98–101*

(This scene has been arranged to make Dorimant jealous. The interruption of the 'three ill-fashioned fellows' is a timely reminder that there are worse social offences than foppishness.)

Who is watching whom and what are they looking for?

(h) *The dialogue between Dorimant alias Mr Courtage and Lady Woodvill on pp 103–4*

Do you agree that Lady Woodvill's false step is that she has allowed her deep distrust of Dorimant to be seen; and so she is made to look foolish for her unfashionable disingenuousness?

(i) *Act IV scene i from Dorimant's aside in the middle of p 107 to the dance on p 112*

What tactics do Harriet and Dorimant use in their battle of wits?

Is Sir Fopling's attitude to women approved of?

(j) *Dorimant's exchange with Mrs Loveit on pp 125–30*

Why does he imitate Sir Fopling?

Why does Mrs Loveit defend fools? (i.e. men less perfect wits than Dorimant.)

Why is Dorimant especially offended by Mrs Loveit's choice of Sir Fopling? And how does he want *her* to clear *his* name?

(k) *The dialogue between Harriet and Dorimant on p 135*

Why is Harriet especially determined not to declare her love unambiguously?

DISCUSSION

(a) See (d) below and Arnold Kettle on attitudes to French cultural influences.

(b) Dorimant's sophistication invents a false division here. His 'honesty' is intended to be cruel; good manners would have softened the blow. Mrs Loveit is surely right when she says 'Now you begin to show yourself'.

(c) Harriet's genuine anger at being expected to dress so unnaturally for a suitor she does not want is neatly contrasted with the anger Young Bellair – a conventional young man with conventional expectations – expects her to display: a tantrum at not being able to attract him even though she does not want him. But Harriet uses her artifices more deliberately than that: she enjoys 'the dear pleasure of dissembling' (p 81).

(d) At the end of Act III scene iii Dorimant and Medley suggest that Sir Fopling may pass 'for a wit' with many. They are themselves such perfectionists that anyone who falls short of their ideal of a genuine wit has to be derided. The concept of a 'wit' is not easy to translate into modern terms. A wit (as well as being witty) is well-dressed, well-bred and well-behaved and especially punctilious in his dealings with the women he seduces. A possible modern equivalent is the person who knows him or herself to be perfectly superior to the fashions and opinions of the colour supplements. You might think that a 'wit' and a 'man of mode' were synonymous, but they were not – quite. This play is very disparaging about the foppish imitation of French manners and the use of French phrases, and thus confirms the satirical edge of the play's title. (Indeed, mode and modish applied to fashion are words that we can only use sarcastically today.) But I have already suggested that Dorimant is the Man of Mode. (See p 44.) I mean that the assessment of himself as the perfect wit (which he shares with most of the other characters in the play) is questioned by Etherege, who suggests that he is really more 'modish' than he knows. Dorimant is in the position of a man who thinks he is unaffected and does not know how affected such an attitude makes him. His streak of cruelty, his determination not to let his composure slip and his discreet and clever handling of his amorous affairs are all more conventional than he knows. Perhaps Sir Fopling comes too close for comfort. This seems to me to be confirmed by the exchange between Harriet and Young Bellair on p 92 (passage e). It may also enlarge your understanding of what 'wit' was in this period if you think of the special wittiness of metaphysical and (later) Augustan poetry. A later Augustan, Alexander Pope, defined wit as ' . . .Nature to advantage dressed, What oft was thought, but ne'er so well expressed.' (*Essay on Criticism*, 1711.)

(f)   We noticed in the first scene that a man of such epicurean taste as Dorimant will require a specially talented wife, and Harriet is herself a 'wit'.

One of the most important items in the code of the wit is that genuine emotions must never be revealed because they are beyond the powers of self-control. So Harriet and Dorimant establish how far Harriet is prepared to go in a series of elaborate metaphors because the real question (whether she will be seduced, or how close she will allow herself to come to it) is too brutal to be faced directly by such sophisticated people. Harriet tries to disentangle herself from the conversation when Dorimant oversteps the mark and refers to her too directly. It is clear from their detailed mimicry of one another that superficially at least they know each other very well already, though this is their first meeting. But Harriet was able to imitate Dorimant much earlier, as Foggy Nan reports. They have studied one another's habits as closely as a hunter watches the quarry.

(g)   This wary mutual observation is emphasized again in the scene Mrs Loveit puts on to deceive Dorimant. So highly controlled is the behaviour of all present that great expertise is required to detect any real feeling beneath the artifice.

(j)   Dorimant is as deeply disturbed by Mrs Loveit's choice of a man he despises to provoke his jealousy as he is by any other event in the play. Her choice impugns his taste. He pretends – or is perhaps his feeling genuine here? – that he, not she, is the wronged party in all this, and in order to restore his reputation, demands that she should publicly humiliate Sir Fopling. His status would be damaged if his cast-off mistress were seen to associate with a fool! At last Mrs Loveit discovers the strength to refuse him.

(k)   To have access to the innermost feelings of another person is to have power over that person. This almost superstitious belief underlies the code of manners and wit which idealized personal composure.

Although it is impossible to account for this attitude accurately, I think it is clear that plays such as *The Man of Mode* in this respect display a very marked reaction to the period of the Civil War and the Interregnum. Deliberate emotional anonymity has become a cult after a period in which intense personal beliefs had contributed to a vast social upheaval. For all their specious freedoms, the people in this play are really very reserved and private, and high feeling is not just an offence to good taste but is ultimately a threat to the still precarious stability of the Restored monarchy.

Religious language

Look at:

Mrs Loveit's description of Dorimant on p 69;

her imprecation at the bottom of p 76;

Harriet and Dorimant's joke about Lent and Easter on p 94;

Lady Woodvill's description of Dorimant on p 95;

Harriet's quick interjection to prevent Dorimant swearing too much on p 136;

and Old Bellair's definition of the marriage ceremony on p 137

These are only a few of the instances where religious language and religious topics are to be found within the play. Even those who hate Dorimant see him as a kind of fallen angel – a trivialization that must have made Milton turn in the grave he had gone to only a couple of years before. The clergyman (Mr Smirk) is a figure of fun, and marriage no more than a license that allows 'a young couple to go to bed together a-God's name'. Harriet neatly indicates that the proper level of commitment in any reasonably serious undertaking is devout but not fanatical: this is of a piece with the general feeling against extremes that we noticed in the previous section.

We do not expect religion to be treated seriously in a comedy, but we might expect that it would not be treated at all. What does this use of religious references suggest to you? I discussed this point on p 42, and with the extra evidence we have just looked at you can now assess my opinions there more judiciously.

Ladies beware Ladies

In Middleton's play we saw how he showed that the immoral demands of men tend to set women against each other. In this play Etherege examines the same dilemma. In a society where women can only achieve status by marriage or more dangerously by clandestine sexual relationships a woman has very little real power over her own life and is forced to compete with other women. I would not want to call this play 'realistic' as Salgado does (p 30) but the predicaments of Mrs Loveit and Belinda are scrutinized with a serious attention to the very real misery that a man like Dorimant may cause which temporarily threatens the comic mood. Our television dramatization, which excludes the broader comic scenes of the play, shows how sombre much of it is.

Read Act II scene ii, and Act V scene i. The servant, Pert (i.e. 'to the point'), sees how these ladies are used as clearly as Foggy Nan does in the first scene. It is an ancient comic tradition that servants, who know what goes on behind the polite and polished facade, enjoy a freedom their masters and mistresses do not have. We have already noticed Dorimant's sophistry that honesty, not cruelty, makes him treat Mrs Loveit so harshly and his clever strategy that puts her at fault for favouring a fool and thus damaging *his* reputation.

Why has she allowed herself to be so hopelessly trapped?

And why does Belinda continue to move towards her own seduction even though she has seen Dorimant use Mrs Loveit so callously?

We saw in the first scene that Dorimant's long-term plans included all the young women in the play, including the serious Emilia. It is she who speaks most generously of him in an interesting exchange on p 84. Though of course Belinda derides him partly to safeguard her reputation it is a real part of her hopelessly divided self that says 'Had you seen him use Mrs Loveit as I have done, you would never indure him more'. And now even Emilia is heading for the trap. But within a page Belinda has agreed to her own seduction.

When she is bundled out of Dorimant's rooms with the dirty bed-linen Belinda is automatically taken by the chairmen to Mrs Loveit's house. Beneath the farcical aspects of this lies a sharp estimation of Dorimant's indifference.

Maybe you thought Belinda and Mrs Loveit very stupid and so in some respects they are. But consider how clearly Etherege shows that the cards are stacked against them: it enhances Dorimant's reputation to be known as a womanizer, but Belinda would suffer complete social ostracism if the truth about her were known. Yet both are equally driven by their sexuality. Belinda cannot resist Dorimant. The fatal mistake that Mrs Loveit makes is that she cannot control her feelings. Instead of putting on a brave face (as she vainly attempts to do with Sir Fopling) she allows Dorimant (and the rest of the world) to see that she is torn by hatred and desire. Such strong and undisguised emotion is very shocking to such a well-mannered society.

In the last scene, Belinda escapes exposure by the skin of her teeth. But Mrs Loveit must bear the additional slight of Harriet's scorn: 'Mr Dorimant has been your God almighty long enough, 'tis time to think of another' (p 143). What Harriet does not know is that Belinda has been to bed with Dorimant and her ignorance of this threatens the balance of power that she and Dorimant appear to achieve at the end of the play, where the question of whether this relationship can survive away from the artificial pleasures of the town is also raised. Surely this is very far from the conventional 'happy ending' described by Salgado on p 22.

A changing culture

EXERCISE

Did the comedies of the Restoration simply start again from the point they had reached when the theatres closed in 1642? The question is hardly fair since you have not studied any earlier comedy; but you should look once again at Salgado's discussion of this point in the first section of the 'Introduction' on pp 11–25. Although you cannot be expected to provide an independent assessment of the development of comedy over our period, you should be able to list some of the changes in society since the beginning of our period which this play helps us identify.

DISCUSSION

Plays like this addressed themselves to the relatively small social group that they mirror. Eventually plays not very unlike this would run foul of the Church because of their general profanity, but on the whole *The Man of Mode* is carefully conservative. The power struggle is played amongst private people who all know the rules of the game even if they cannot all keep to them. The dimension of public power over private lives represented by the Duke in *Women Beware Women* is completely missing here. Yet Dorimant is a satiric parody of Hobbesian political theory: his sexual attractiveness and intelligence are the sources of his power to manipulate to his own ends the society in which he lives. The crucial difference is that these people *seem* to take lightly what in the earlier play was serious and prominent: 'business' in *The Man of Mode* is no more than a euphemism for the pursuit of women (see for example p 73). But of course if the woman in question possesses a fortune which will become her husband's property when she marries then 'business' is real business, as commercially important as the trading which takes Leantio away from Bianca. Young Bellair and Emilia have to gain the approval of their parents or forfeit their fortunes. Harriet, in a rebellious mood, would like to fling caution to the winds: 'Shall I be paid down by a covetous parent for a purchase? I need no land; no, I'll lay myself out all in love.' (p 80)

Dorimant on the other hand never loses sight of her fortune. He says to Young Bellair:

> The wise will find a difference in our fate,
> You wed a woman, I a good estate.

Thus Harriet's fortune will protect him from the damage to his reputation that an emotional relationship would entail as well as repair him financially. In *Women Beware Women* money was made; here it is married. This was a period in which the competition for rich heiresses was particularly fierce because of the Royalists' wish to restore estates confiscated during the Interregnum (see *C of R* pp 172–5 and *Three Restoration Comedies* 'Introduction' p 22). It is worth noting that Harriet is *not* a rich merchant's daughter but comes from a landed family: her money is very well-bred. You have looked long enough at the treatment of the women in the play to be able to evaluate their relative status at the end of our period of study in so far as a play can show it. Like all the other political issues which lie under the play, this too is obscured by an artful display of good manners. Perhaps the greatest change which this play reveals is that in it we can see an image of a society which has learned the wisdom of keeping its most ardent feelings discreetly covered.

In *Women Beware Women* the Cardinal reminds his brother the Duke that adultery will be punished by eternal damnation (Act IV scene i); in *The Man of Mode* adultery is a theme for comedy. Religion itself, which had been interwoven amongst the causes of the Civil War, is in this play hardly more than an ornament of fashionable speech. *The Man of Mode* is not a realistic picture of any part of post-Restoration society; but surely it is a very accurate rendering of a post-Restoration fantasy – of a society taking a holiday from moral responsibility.

References

Hill, Christopher (1980, revised edition) *The Century of Revolution*, Nelson. (*C of R*)

Salgado, Gamini (ed) (1968) *Three Restoration Comedies*, Penguin (Set book).

Architecture: Caroline Style and Stuart Cultural Policy

Contents

Architecture: Caroline Style and Stuart Cultural Policy

Introduction

In 1980 the Bank of England issued a £50 note bearing the image of Sir Christopher Wren. If it means anything to talk about an 'English national architect', Wren would stand a good chance for the nomination. His character and accomplishments well suit our image of the modest, common-sensical, all-round intellect, eschewing excess and solving problems as they arise. He was astronomer, mathematician, biologist, classicist and a founder member of the Royal Society. And his buildings fix many of the contours of our national consciousness – St Paul's and the City churches, Chelsea and Greenwich hospitals, his contributions to Oxford, Cambridge and the Middle Temple. Who will forget the photographs of St Paul's wreathed in smoke during the Blitz, a symbol for the survival of Englishness in the holocaust (*Plate 1*)? (All the plates referred to are contained in Illustration Book 2.)

Wren's is a dangerous legend to tinker with. We see Wren's work partly through the filter of the dreadfully named *Wrenaissance* of the first quarter of this century. During the deeply isolationist withdrawal from European culture after the First World War, hundreds of post offices, banks and commercial and municipal buildings were erected in a style which claimed Wren as its figurehead. And it was during the nineteen-twenties that the twenty Wren Society volumes were published, commemorating the drawings, documents and images of Wren's buildings in exhaustive detail. Ironically, part of the effect of this intensive research was to place Wren's achievement more precisely into its context, stripping many hundreds of false attributions from the catalogue of his works and revealing clearly the importance of his contemporaries. It is now quite obvious that the one thing Wren did not create was the 'Wren style', as it is popularly understood. This was a collective achievement by an assortment of builders, craftsmen, surveyors and gentleman architects, of whom Wren was perhaps the most important, but not the most innovatory.

I hope to show how a coherent and unified style came to replace the bewildering array of eclectic styles characteristic of the 'artisan mannerism' of the Jacobean period. In doing so, I will try to show that radical changes were affecting the building professions, while the evolution of the professional architect as a specialist intermediary between builders and patrons was slowly coming about. I will also look for the sources of this style, both among foreign influences, notably Dutch and French, and in the structure of contacts between craftsmen and architects which modulated the transmission of ideas during our period.

My second aim is to assess the objectives of Stuart cultural policy during the Surveyorship of Christopher Wren. Did Charles II and James II pick up again the ambitious projects of their father? To what extent was Charles II trying to emulate the example of Louis XIV? In answering these questions, we will look at a very specific selection of Wren's work, concentrating on the monumental secular commissions. This view is broadened considerably in Television programmes 12 and 13, where the rebuilding of London after the Fire and St Paul's are considered. In Radio programme 13, the operation of the Office of Works and its effects will be investigated.

The Caroline style and its sources

To understand how a unified style of architecture evolves, we must see how ideas and practices are communicated across a wide range of craftsmen, 'experts' and patrons. Ideas really spread through contacts. What distinguishes the second from the first half of the seventeenth century is the greater range and interplay of these contacts. Increasingly, provincial craftsmen began to work with people (patrons, architects) whose ideas had been moulded in London. And emerging from these craftsmen was a generation of men who had the ambition (and resources), to rise in status to that of 'architect'. Sculptors (in wood and stone), masons, bricklayers, carpenters, plasterers and glaziers began to acquire the skills of the draughtsman and surveyor and to design their own buildings. Furthermore, their buildings are in a similar style to those of the specialized surveyors and architects. The sharp contrast, which we noted in Block 2, between the architecture of Inigo Jones (and his few admirers) and the 'artisan mannerism' of City or country masons, no longer applies to the same extent after the sixteen-fifties. We must begin by looking at the status and aspirations of the different kinds of people who designed these buildings.

Architects, builders, craftsmen, gentlemen

The modern notion of an architect is one which attributes complete control in the design process to a man or firm. The builders and craftsmen carry out the construction according to precisely prepared instructions and measured drawings.

In the sixteenth and seventeenth centuries, the design work tended to be shared between a number of people, from the client to the craftsmen and contractors themselves who were commissioned to carry out the work. As a result many Elizabethan and Jacobean buildings betray all too obviously a multiplicity of styles in their form and decoration, since no one person was really in charge of the whole.

With Inigo Jones, the Smythsons and others, however, the Italian Renaissance concept of the architect began to assert itself – one in which one man conceives, details and supervises construction according to a set of plans and instructions. An early eighteenth-century definition makes this transition explicit:

> *Architect*: a master-workman in a building: 'tis also sometimes taken for the *Surveyor* of a building, viz. he that designs the Model, or draws the plot, or Draught, of the whole Fabrick; whose business it is to consider of the whole manner and method of the building and also the Charge and Expence . . . The drawing of draughts is most commonly the work of a Surveyor tho' there be many Master-workmen that will contrive a building, and draw a draught, or design thereof, as well as most (and better than some) surveyors.
> (T. N. 'Philomath' *The City and Country Purchaser and Builder's Directory*, London, 1703. Quoted in Colvin, 1975.)

The emergence of the profession of architect or surveyor owed a great deal to changes in the method of contracting for building work. Sir Christopher Wren described the alternatives:

> There are 3 ways of working: by the day, by measure, by great; if by the day it tells me when they are lazy. If by measure it gives me light on every particular, and tells me what I am to provide. If by the great I can make a sure bargain neither to be overreached nor to hurt the undertaker [building contractor]: for in things they are not every day used to, they do often injure themselves, and when they begin to find it, they shuffle and slight the work to save themselves. I think the best way in this business is to work by measure: according to the prices in the estimate or lower if you can, and measure the work at 3 or 4 measurements as it rises. But you must have an understanding, trusty Measurer; there are few that are skilled in measuring stone work, I have bred up 2 or 3.
> (Letter to Bishop of Oxford, 1681.)

53

This needs a little explanation. 'By the day' means direct labour: the workmen were paid day rates (while they were working) and the client had to find the materials himself and take all the economic risk of non-completion or excess spending. This had been a common practice until this period and continued as the normal way of employing labourers for digging foundations, erecting scaffolding and assisting the masons and bricklayers. At the other extreme, 'by the great' involved a devolution of responsibility and risk to the contractors. The client would agree a once and for all contract with the various tradesmen, or with one contractor who would subcontract the other work. A contract for Holme Lacey, Herefordshire (1673–4), bound the mason, Anthony Deane, 'to do all the Mason's, Carpenter's and Bricklayer's work, tyling and paving only excepted' for £1,645.14.10d. Hugh May (the architect) was to arbitrate in case of a dispute. This meant that Deane would himself subcontract the brick and woodwork, since he was a stone mason by trade. The dangers in this system are indicated in Wren's letter. Masons might undertake more than they could deliver, either through incompetence or in a calculated attempt to win a contract which they hoped the client would later amend to cover the remaining work to be completed.

'By measure' therefore represented a compromise. Those commissioning the building were protected from lazy workmen by making payments conditional on a specified quality and quantity of construction. On the other hand the contractors were protected from taking all the risk for a very large contract in one bite. In practice, payment would be spaced out into half a dozen or more 'measurements'. The consequence was that a skilled surveyor was necessary to 'measure' the work and mediate between client and contractor, and this mediation increasingly came to cover the specialized task of preparing the measured drawings for the design of the building. Now, it is this skill of draughtsmanship which prepares the ground for the modern specialist architect. Once a man can design a whole building on paper, and can rely on builders capable of interpreting these drawings, the specialization of functions can become real.

We should not exaggerate the role of the surveyor-architect, however. It was quite usual for a client to approach someone known for his talent in architectural design, and commission a plan of a building which would then be put to a team of craftsmen for contract. The 'architect' would retain some control of the design, but would effectively allow the craftsmen not only to design the details of woodwork, plaster and so forth, but also to modify aspects of the masonry and overall form of the building as occasion and their taste dictated.

Sharing the risk between client and contractor presupposed a fairly healthy building industry. Only masons and craftsmen with the assets or credit to survive for months or years at a time without payment – until the next 'measurement' – could benefit from this system. The seventeenth century marked a general improvement in conditions for contractors as landed and commercial wealth began to be invested in building. A number of mason contractors became extremely wealthy, especially after the Great Fire of 1666, and it was their resources which made possible the construction of so many buildings in so short a space of time. For example, between 1670 and 1690, a total of some £150,000 in contracts for the City Churches was shared out between just over fifteen principal contractors and another £70,000 worth went to the same people on contracts for the Royal Palaces. At St Paul's these same firms handled £143,000 in contracts (1675–1700) in addition to over £100,000 in material.

The rise of the mason-contractor also entailed the breaking down of many of the Guild barriers which had restricted mobility and ambitions in the Middle Ages. The Companies (Masons', Carpenters', Tylers' and Bricklayers', Joiners', Carvers', Painter-Stainers' and Plasterers') still exercised a monopoly in their respective trades, although this monopoly was increasingly threatened. The Masons' Company, for example, had the right to search for 'false' work (defective craftsmanship). Furthermore all Purbeck stone imported into London was supposed to be 'searched' by the Masons'

Company and the 'search fees' provided a substantial source of income for the Company. The Masons also pursued members of other trades who either hindered the completion of masonry work or prevented the necessary standards being reached.

The main threat to the economic viability of the Companies was the competition of 'foreignors' – craftsmen or contractors from the provinces or London suburbs who escaped the onerous duties which the Companies imposed on their members. Just as the City itself was suffering from the reluctance of merchants to take on the unpaid duties of Alderman and Councillor, so the Companies were discovering that the prestige of adopting the Company Livery and serving as Assistant, Warden or Master was becoming insufficient to counterbalance the entry fees and loss of profits resulting from the work involved. Television programme 12 shows how this problem was exacerbated by the growth of the suburbs, and especially the west end, where many merchants and craftsmen were choosing to live, outside the control of the City. Again and again the various Companies collaborated in petitions to the City calling for a stop to the employment of 'foreign' labour. The situation became much more serious after the Great Fire, when the Rebuilding Acts of 1667 and 1670 empowered 'foreign' craftsmen to work freely on the reconstruction of London, until the work was finished; additionally after seven years they became automatically entitled to freedom of the appropriate Company. A very large number of successful provincial craftsmen (like Christopher Kempster) took advantage of this opportunity, although some did choose to enter the Companies immediately 'by redemption', on payment of a sum of money.

EXERCISE

What consequences can you see in the loosening of control by the Company Guilds?

DISCUSSION

First, mobility encouraged the exchange of ideas. While the most influential masons had remained in London protected by the Masons' Company, the spread of new ideas was bound to be limited. Secondly, the building boom of the seventeenth century allowed mason-contractors to make their fortunes, provided that they could move freely to where the demand was greatest. After the Fire, it was clear to everyone that the 'foreignors' would have to be allowed in to London, or the City would never be rebuilt. In stylistic terms, the conservative spirit of the Guilds was bound to hamper innovation, while the mobile contractor, who probably worked with several different architects or patrons, was able to profit from the experience. Finally, the rise of the mobile mason-contractor with substantial capital reinforced the emergence of the specialist 'professional' architect, interceding between client and builder.

EXERCISE

Look at *Plates 2–20 and 81–2*. Before investigating these buildings in any detail, look through them briefly, noting dates, places and architects. Can you see a clear historical development from first to last or do they all look broadly similar? Can you guess which of the designers are in fact professional architects (i.e. they made their living designing buildings) and which are sculptors, builders, scientists or gentlemen amateurs? Can you identify Court as opposed to country or City clients for the houses?

DISCUSSION

I hope that you agree with me in concluding that these buildings are broadly similar. There are a number of points which might be made about the stylistic development between the sixteen-thirties and 1700, but this selection of illustrations does not bring them out. The reasons for this will be laid out below. All the houses are well-proportioned, elegant but simple. Some have an applied order (*Plates 7, 8, 10*) but most do not. I don't think that you could guess what kind of person designed each house. In fact, the 'architects' come from very diverse backgrounds, as we will see. Similarly, the Court clients cannot be easily distinguished from the country gentlemen.

Only John Webb and Christopher Wren are 'architects' in the sense that their prime occupation was designing and supervising the construction of buildings. Nicholas Stone and William Stanton both came from families of masons. They both ran large sculpture workshops, but also practised as mason-contractors and, occasionally, as architects. Sir Roger Pratt and Hugh May were gentlemen architects, designing houses for friends in the country or at Court, but not dependent on architecture for their income. As we'll see, however, May did earn part of his living from Crown appointments to architectural positions after the sixteen-sixties. Robert Hooke was a scientist, a mainstay of the Royal Society. From the sixteen-seventies onwards, he spent more and more time assisting his friend Wren on the supervision of the rebuilding of London. Of the clients involved, William Lowndes, who built Winslow Hall, was secretary to the Treasury from 1699 to 1702, and the Earl of Clarendon is well known to you. Of the others, some were courtiers, like Sir John Shaw, and the others cover a broad spectrum of affiliations.

I hope this preliminary survey substantiates the general point that the seventeenth century witnessed the coming together of Court and country styles in domestic architecture. To see how it came about, we must go back to the Inigo Jones circle in the sixteen-thirties.

The Jonesian tradition and the spread of classicism

To understand why the general consensus of architectural opinion came to favour classicism, we must begin with the legacy of Inigo Jones. His pupil, John Webb (1611–72) is the prototype of the professional architect. After leaving the Merchant Taylors School in 1628, he became assistant to Inigo Jones, to whom he was related. He learnt about classical architecture from Jones, and became a competent draughtsman. He inherited many of Jones's drawings, as well as his library of architectural books and his collection of Palladio's drawings. Despite a short period of imprisonment, Webb was able to practice throughout the Interregnum, in the Palladian style of his master. His association with the masons and craftsmen who built these houses (especially Edward Marshall, see p 57) helped to educate a generation into the Palladian style.

In Block 2, we looked at the Queen's House, Greenwich, and the Prince's Lodging, Newmarket, both by Inigo Jones (Illustration Book 1, *Plates 22, 71 and 21*). We also included Raynham Hall (Illustration Book 1, *Plate 20*) in a style heavily indebted to Jones and perhaps owing something to his actual intervention. John Webb built up a lively country house practice during the Interregnum, following these lines. For Chaloner Chute, he redesigned the interiors and added a classical portico to The Vyne (1654–6) (*Plate 7*). For Sir John Maynard, he built Gunnersbury House (*Plate 8*) (*c. 1658–63*), now demolished.

EXERCISE

Look at *Plates 7–9*. In what ways, do you think these two houses could be described as 'Jonesian' or 'Palladian'? Refer back to Block 2 if you need to revise these terms.

DISCUSSION

The Vyne is a useful indicator, since it shows precisely how simple a transformation could be achieved by the addition of a classical portico to an earlier house. The portico not only serves to mark the entrance as clearly as possible, but also to suggest 'nobility'. Palladio explains in the *Four Books of Architecture* (Venice, 1570) that porticos originated in domestic architecture before being taken over for temples by the ancient Greeks and Romans. But the symbolism worked the other way in the Renaissance – clients associated their houses with sacred and monumental building by adding porticos to essentially simple boxes. Gunnersbury House is a classical invocation of Palladian villa architecture. The house reads as a well-proportioned box whose only ornament is a large portico raised on a high basement. You are meant to realize that the portico is the external signal for a large and splendid room inside. These houses are classical, then, in that they are well-proportioned and clear expressions of a single design idea. They are Palladian in so far as Palladio was the architect who perfected the 'cube-plus-portico' formula.

In Palladio's most prestigious examples, such as the Villa Rotonda (*Plate 21*) another element of sacred symbolism is added – the dome. This model – a cube with four porticos and a dome – was not going to be copied in Britain until the full-scale Palladian revival of the Burlington group in the early eighteenth century. But the idea of a monumental dome, lined up behind a portico in the middle of a facade, was to linger at the back of architects' minds. Webb and Wren both used it in their Palace designs *(Plates 70, 75)*.

The Jones-Webb tradition percolated through the architectural and building world by a number of channels. For example, Inigo Jones probably advised the Pratts on Coleshill House *(Plates 3–6)* especially the interiors. The combination of richly decorated interior and rather simple exterior became the norm for the more ambitious architect and builder. Secondly, Webb's very full career in the sixteen-fifties and sixties introduced a number of influential masons and craftsmen to the Jonesian manner. The mason of Gunnersbury House and The Vyne, for example, was Edward Marshall (1598–1675). Marshall had worked with Nicholas Stone (cf. *Plate 2*) in his youth, as a sculptor. He built up a successful practice in funerary sculpture and was able to win the position of Master Mason to the Crown in 1660, passing this position on to his son Joshua Marshall in 1673.

Joshua Marshall (1629–78) built six of the City churches and the Monument and was one of the two main mason-contractors at St Paul's in the early stages. So the Marshall family form an unbroken line between the Inigo Jones tradition and the Wren period. It is important to realize, too, that like most stone masons, the Marshalls' yard at Fetter Lane combined sculpture with building. Without a steady business in funerary monuments (*Plate 22*), which, like some architectural embellishments, could be worked on in all weathers and throughout the winter, a mason would have difficulty acquiring enough revenue to support the financial risk of large masonry contracts. The Marshalls' style was a robust form of English realism, unlike the more spectacular undercutting effects of the Dutch-influenced carvers we will look at later (*Plates 33 and 80*).

Another direct link between the Jones-Webb tradition and the Restoration period is the Stone workshop. Nicholas Stone (1583–1647) came from a family of Devon quarrymen, a profession which characterizes a number of successful masons of the new type. By the twenties he had built up a successful practice as sculptor (*Plate 43*). Inigo Jones picked him to build the Banqueting House (Illustration Book 1, *Plates 56–60 and 74–5*) and had him appointed Master Mason at Windsor (1626) and Master Mason to the King in 1632. It was this experience which enabled Stone to design the middle wing of Cornbury House as early as 1632–3 (*Plate 2*) in a Jonesian style which matches that of Hugh May thirty years later. Nicholas's son John Stone (1620–67) was brought up as a gentleman, educated at Westminster School, where Wren, Hooke and Dryden also went. And it was in the Stone workshop that Caius Gabriel Cibber (1630–1700) came to work in the sixteen-fifties. We'll come back to Cibber's work later.

The important point to learn from the Stone family story is that masons were not only able to achieve gentleman status in one generation, but were also able to travel abroad and bring back the best of Dutch, Italian and French ideas. Nicholas Stone had worked in Amsterdam with the City mason, Hendrik de Keyser, and had married de Keyser's daughter. Members of de Keyser's family worked in London, with the Stones and on their own account. John Stone, not surprisingly, kept up these contacts and helped to introduce the Dutch fashion of hyper-realistic carving of garlands of fruit and flowers, which influenced all British craftsmanship to some extent in the sixteen-sixties.

Furthermore, the architectural style practised in Holland throughout the sixteen-fifties and sixties helped to form a bridge between Inigo Jones and the Restoration period. Hendrik de Keyser (1565–1621) and Jacob van Campen (1595–1657) had been transforming the mannerism of their traditional national sytle into an elegant and dignified Palladianism.

Dutch Palladianism

The Town House (now the Royal Palace), Amsterdam, designed by van Campen, on which a whole generation of Dutch craftsmen worked (*Plates 23–4*) was well known. John Stone actually worked on it. The internal sculptural decoration was admired for its realistic treatment. Externally, the rows of superimposed orders are rather unimaginative. Note the lantern, a half-hearted reference to Palladio's portico-dome idea.

Van Campen's Mauritshuis in the Hague (*Plate 25*), built in 1633–5, set a new ideal, using a giant order of pilasters (rectangular columns) framing two storeys of pedimented windows. Prince Maurice of Nassau, the client, could afford more decorative embellishment than most Dutch patrons, and we find here an abundance of the favourite festoons and swags, with very realistic flowers and fruit, which so influenced English sculptors and masons.

At a more modest level, de Keyser's Coymanshuis in Amsterdam, 1625 (*Plate 26*), showed English architects how to use superimposed orders of pilasters in straightforward brick street architecture. This facade can be read as a basement supporting an ionic and corinthian order of pilasters, surmounted by an attic, but the logic of regular, well proportioned apertures with almost no wall space in between makes for a convincing city architecture. The rebuilding of London after the Fire, and the regulations which Wren and his colleagues framed to control it, owes a great deal to Dutch examples like this.

Pieter Post's Huis ten Bosch near the Hague, 1645–51 (*Plate 27*), sums up these Dutch characteristics. This house, which is contemporary with Coleshill (*Plates 3–6*), shows that Dutch architects were working in a parallel direction to Pratt and his English contemporaries.

The English architect who brought over the purest interpretation of the new Dutch Palladianism was Hugh May. Eltham Lodge (*Plates 10–12*) was built for Sir John Shaw, a Royalist who had supported the exiled Court during the Interrugnum, and won out in the Restoration with a knighthood and the gift of a customs farm. May introduced for the applied portico the giant order of pilasters of the Mauritshuis, but did not carry the order round the facade. The plan (*Plate 11*) shows a variation on the Pratt double pile, with a large Hall behind the temple front portico, and staircases to right and left of the central corridor. The main staircase (*Plate 12*) is a miracle of craftsmanship, with panels of pine, pierced and carved in full relief. Eltham Lodge and the remodelling of Cassiobury for the Earl of Essex (1674–6) (which also employed a giant order of applied pilasters), formed the basis for a courtier style which might have been identifiable as distinctly 'Royalist', given the greater ambition of the use of the applied order. But May's style in fact merged into the dominant forms of Pratt's a-stylar domestic manner (i.e. not using columns or pilasters), and it is difficult to make any identification of style with political affiliations along these lines.

EXERCISE

Having looked at these Dutch examples, look again at the English houses in *Plates 2–20*. What useful comparisons occur to you?

DISCUSSION

The similarity between the Mauritshuis *(Plate 25)* and Eltham Lodge *(Plate 10)* is quite striking. There is the same restrained use of an applied portico, clear articulation of wall surfaces and selective use of applied decoration. The Huis ten Bosch *(Plate 27),* on the other hand, typifies the kind of a-stylar brick architecture which dominated British and Dutch domestic building in the second half of the seventeenth century. The plan type, with projecting wings forming a clear massing of forms, was the same as that used at Clarendon House *(Plate 13)* and Belton *(Plate 16).* The general conclusion must be that English and Dutch domestic architecture developed in similar ways.

The Dutch connection was not only made by craftsmen like the Stone family. A number of gentry, often Royalists, had taken refuge in the Netherlands during the Interregnum. This is one factor which effectively blurs the distinction between the Dutch and French influences on British architecture. For, although the architecture of Louis XIV's Court only had an influence on Court architects, as we will see, Dutch architecture formed the basic style of domestic architecture for Court and country alike, and for Tory and Whig gentry. You might like to contrast this with the general points made by J. R. Jones in 'Britain and Europe in the Seventeenth Century' (Reader, article 4). Three examples of gentleman architects will show how foreign influences reached this country.

Gentleman architects

Roger Pratt (1620–85) was probably the most important of the gentleman architects. Wealthy enough to afford to study law but not to practice it, he was also able to spend six years on a study tour of the continent – a trip which coincided with the Civil War. Sharing lodgings with John Evelyn in Rome, he was able to learn a great deal about architectural theory, building up an important library of books. On his return in 1649, he began to advise his friends and relatives on architectural matters, in the manner described in his 'Certain heads to be largely treated of concerning the undertaking of any building'.

> If you be not able to handsomely contrive it yourself, get some ingenious gentleman who has seen much of that kind abroad and been somewhat versed in the best authors of architecture: viz. Palladio, Scamozzi, Serlio, etc. [Italian Renaissance architectural writers] to do it for you, and to give you a design of it in paper, though but roughly drawn, which will generally fall out better than one which shall be given you by a home-bred Architect for want of his better experience, as is daily seen.
>
> (Gunther, *The Architecture of Sir Roger Pratt,* p 60.)

Pratt himself valued the experience of good examples 'of that kind abroad', as well as the 'best authors'. But the importance of Coleshill House *(Plates 3–6)* and Clarendon House *(Plate 13)* was the subtle adaptation of Dutch, French and Italian influences to English conditions. It is significant too, that Pratt's sphere of influence was distinct from the Court.

Hugh May (1621–84), on the other hand, was more derivative in his style and more limited in his appeal. During the Interregnum, May had the tricky task of acting as the Duke of Buckingham's agent in England, raising money from the sale of pictures in York House and looking after valuable properties. In 1656, May went with the painter Lely to Holland, to join the Court in exile. In 1660 he was rewarded with a position in the Office of Works, as Paymaster (then Comptroller, after 1668). Disappointed in obtaining the Surveyor General's post after Denham's death, he was nevertheless compensated financially with a pension of £300 and, later, two lucrative government sinecures. He later took over as Comptroller of the Works at Windsor Palace, and carried out a superb suite of rooms in the Upper Ward

(Plates 63, 64, 83). It says a great deal for Charles II's judgement that he was able to advance Christopher Wren to the Surveyorship, above men like May, Webb and Pratt, while still giving these architects scope for their talents.

May was one of the experts asked to advise on the repair of Old St Paul's, and served with Wren and Pratt as Commissioner for supervising the rebuilding of London. He designed a sequence of influential country houses for the leading courtiers of the Restoration, employing Grinling Gibbons and Verrio to carry out lavish interiors. His exterior style, however, was reserved and discreet, following the example of Dutch architects like van Campen *(Plate 10)*.

Another Royalist gentleman architect was Captain William Winde. Winde's career followed a by now familiar pattern. He was born in Holland, after his Royalist father had taken refuge there from the Civil War. Returning in 1660 to claim the family estates, Winde tried to succeed as a soldier and military engineer. Despite favourable remarks from the King, advancement eluded him, and he turned to architecture as a distraction from his duties in the King's Troop. Friendly with courtiers and men of letters alike, he was well placed to translate the new architectural principles into house designs for the gentry. His supervision of these designs seems to have been fairly casual, and it is clear that he worked harmoniously with a team of master craftsmen, including Edward Pierce, Edward Goudge, William Stanton and Jonathan and Edward Wilcox. The documentation shows that he often gave great initiative to these craftsmen to provide drawings of their own work. In style, his houses follow closely the example set by Roger Pratt and, to a lesser extent, Hugh May. *(Plates 16–17.)* Winde shows the close contacts between masons and gentlemen architects which helped to unify and bind together domestic architecture. For William Stanton, who was the mason who built Belton to Winde's design, himself went on to design Denham Place *(Plates 18, 19)*. Stanton, like Joshua Marshall, came from a family of successful London masons and carried out numerous monuments, of which one is for Sir John Brownlow at Belton (1679) *(Plate 28)*. The Stanton yard in Holborn was probably the biggest in London in the sixteen-seventies and eighties.

Sculpture

We have seen that masons tended to combine sculpture with building, for economic reasons. Part of the glory of seventeenth-century architecture is the wealth of craftsmanship inside and out. One reason for this must be the combination of skills offered by the new breed of successful contractors. The case of Edward Pierce shows the range of skills a sculptor-mason needed.

Edward Pierce (c. 1630–95)

Pierce was a sculptor-mason who worked regularly with William Winde, but his origins were as a painter. He entered the Painter-Stainers' Company in 1656 as his father had done before him, and finished up as Master of the Company just before his death. By the sixteen-sixties he had specialized in sculpture in wood and stone, executing famous busts of Milton (1656), Cromwell and Wren (c. 1673) *(Plate 29)*. He was an accomplished draughtsman *(Plate 30)* and a magnificent carver in wood *(Plate 31)* as well as stone.

After the Fire, he established himself as a mason-contractor, taking on major contracts at St Andrew Holborn, St Clement Danes and St Paul's, where he also took over Joshua Marshall's work after his death. Archbishop Sancroft commissioned him to design and build the Bishop's Palace, Lichfield (1686–7) *(Plate 32)*. Pierce's career is an example of the versatility and mobility of the best craftsmen during this period.

Caius Gabriel Cibber (1630–1700)

Untrained as a sculptor himself, John Stone had relied on Anthony Ellis, his father's best apprentice and on his foreman, one of the most brilliant sculptors of the period, Caius Gabriel Cibber (1630–1700). Cibber's father was cabinet-maker to the King of Denmark, and the young man was sent to Italy to learn his trade as a sculptor. In the fifties and sixties, Cibber managed to establish a reputation so that he was able to take over after John Stone's death in 1667. In addition to some spectacular sculpture, Cibber took on quite large building contracts in the seventies and eighties, and designed and built the Danish Church in Wellclose Square (1694–6, demolished). The Sackville Monument (1677) (*Plates 33, 80*) is perhaps the most spectacular, with its eerie domesticity. The sculptures of Raving and Melancholy Madness (*Plate 34*) which he made to adorn Robert Hooke's Bethlehem Hospital owe something to Michelangelo's Medici Chapel figures, and to the soulful characterizations of Italian Mannerist bronzes. They would be inconceivable without some familiarity with Italian examples. And his relief on The Monument (*Plate 35*), showing Charles II, dressed as a Roman Emperor, comforting the stricken city and inaugurating the great rebuilding programme, makes a good job of translating the whole scene into appropriate allegorical forms. Cibber's sensitive and nervous style combines Italian sources and Dutch technique.

Grinling Gibbons (1648–1721)

Although his parents were English, Gibbons was born in Rotterdam, coming to this country only after the Restoration. Evelyn recounts how he discovered the young man in his cottage at Deptford, carving a wooden relief copy of Tintoretto's 'The Crucifixion'. Through the intervention of John Evelyn and Hugh May, Gibbons found work at the Windsor Office of Works (*Plate 36*). Gibbons benefited from this Royal patronage to build a successful career as statuarist and decorative carver. His statues of Charles II and James II (*Plates 37–8*) capture the bombastic pretentiousness of some art used in the service of European absolutism and his proposed monument for Charles I must take its place in the iconography of the 'martyr' king's mythology (*Plate 39*) alongside Wren's proposed mausoleum (*Plates 59–61*). The altarpiece which Gibbons and Arnold Quellin (son of the famous Dutch sculptor) carved for the Catholic chapel at Whitehall for James II and his Queen survives only as fragments and individual statues (*Plates 40–1*). That this Catholic altarpiece finished up in Westminster Abbey, donated by Queen Anne in 1706, is one of those curious facts which defy precise explanation. The elaborate white marble construction with its purple columns and veined marble pilasters did nothing to allay suspicions about the Catholic activities of the Court.

Unlike Pierce, Gibbons did not diversify into building. Like Wren, he has benefited from an excessive eagerness to attribute almost any high quality work to his chisel. He was undoubtedly one of the most skilful carvers and statuaries of his day, but was able to pick up a tradition already well established in the fifties and sixties. The naturalism of his style (*Plate 42*) has to be located in the Dutch naturalism which characterized the Quellin school. The distance travelled from the sixteen-thirties can be judged by comparing the work of these three sculptors with Nicholas Stone's early work (*Plate 43*).

The other building trades

During the seventeenth century, a gradual move away from timber to brick construction can be identified, especially in domestic architecture. Before 1600, bricklaying was a trade characteristically carried out only in London or those regions where neither stone nor timber were easily available. During the sixteen-thirties, a tradition of brick building began to present new standards of comfort and elegance in the London sphere of influence. Following the 1667 and 1670 Rebuilding Acts, which specified detailed standards of brick construction for fire prevention reasons, brick became a standard for emulation throughout the country. Transport costs usually doubled the price of stone, but, where the clay was suitable, local brick fields could be opened quickly and cheaply, and the investment quickly redeemed.

Although the typical brick buildings of the 'artisan mannerist' type in the middle of the century rivalled stone in the richness and complexity of their detailing, during the fifties a style arose which exploited the dignified simplicity of brick wall surfaces offset by well proportioned classical detailing in stone or stucco. Peter Mills (1598–1670), was one of the first bricklayers to advance to the genuine status of 'architect and surveyor' through his trade. Appointed Bricklayer to the City of London in 1643, he served as Master of the Tylers' and Bricklayers' Company in 1649–60. He built a number of important houses for leading figures during the Interregnum. John Thurloe, Cromwell's Secretary of State, almost certainly commissioned Wisbech Castle, Cambridgeshire from Mills, and Oliver St John (the Chief Justice) built Thorpe Hall, near Peterborough, to Mills's design (1653–4). This house was investigated in Television programme 11. In addition, Mills developed a number of properties in London, privately and in conjunction with City speculators.

Although Mills seems to have been a good republican during the Interregnum, he was commissioned by the City to erect the Triumphal Arches welcoming Charles II in 1661 (*Plates 44–5*). By this time, he had ceased to work as a bricklayer, relinquishing his post as Bricklayer to the City of London (1643–60), to concentrate on the more genteel work of surveyor and architect. The City asked him to act on their behalf in negotiation with the Dean and Chapter of St Paul's during the discussions about the possible repair of the Cathedral. He was one of the three Surveyors appointed by the City to survey the ruins after the Fire and supervise the provisions of the Rebuilding Acts. He was the first choice to build the Royal Exchange, but pleaded overwork on City business. It is clear, in fact, that Mills was the man the City fathers turned to for advice and assistance on all building matters from the sixteen-fifties until his death. It is possible that he was influential in the decision to pass an Act in 1657 specifying that new buildings in London should be of brick or stone. In other words, Mills was an important example of the artisan who chose to 'elevate' his status to that of architect and surveyor.

Another of the men appointed by the City as Surveyor after the Fire had also reached the top in his particular trade – carpentry. Edward Jerman (or Jarman) (? – 1668) came from a family of London carpenters established since the Elizabethan heyday of the profession. He was City Carpenter until 1657, when he resigned, and remained Surveyor of the Fishmongers' Company from 1654 until his death in 1668. By 1666, he was clearly too ill to carry out the arduous surveying work asked of him, but he did design the Royal Exchange (*Plate 46*) and a number of Companies' Halls, including the Weaver's, Drapers', Fishmongers' (*Plate 47*), Mercers' (*Plate 48*) and Wax Chandlers' Halls. His younger brother Roger Jerman was City Carpenter in turn (1662–78). Jerman was less open to the new architectural style than Mills, although he did purge his style of some of the excesses of 'artisan mannerism'.

Christopher Wren (1632–1723)

Wren and Robert Hooke belong to a particular branch of the general category of gentleman architect. Both owed their recognition in Court, and their entry into architecture, to their reputation as intellectuals and scientists. It was Charles's fascination with scientific experiments, watches and observatories which led him to prefer Wren's virtually untested capacities as architect to the claims of Webb, May and Pratt. It's worth looking at Wren's career in a little detail because it brings together many of the themes we have been following in this course.

Wren's origins were characteristic of the gentlemen architects we have looked at so far. His father and uncle were staunch Royalists, Laudian churchmen of some standing in the reigns of James I and Charles I. Wren's father was Rector of East Knoyle in Wiltshire, where Christopher was born in 1632. Two years later the Rev. Christopher Wren took over from his brother as Dean of Windsor, where he stayed until the pillage of the Deanery during the Civil War. The family then removed to Bristol, until the fall of that city, before taking refuge in Bletchingdon with William Holder, who had married Christopher's sister. Holder had been a Fellow at Pembroke and was an intellectual with a keen interest in mathematics and the new learning. Aubrey attributes to his influence the young Wren's first introduction to geometry, arithmetic and the experimental sciences.

In 1641, Wren went to Westminster School, where Dr Busby was creating a reputation for rigorous studies in the classics and in the new sciences. Dryden, Locke and Robert Hooke also passed through Dr Busby's hands at this time. In 1649, Wren went up to Wadham College, Oxford, as a gentleman commoner. By this time, he had already acquired a reputation as a prodigy intellect, and quickly entered the Oxford circle of scientists and thinkers around Dr Wilkins to which you were introduced in Block 8. Wren's particular skills were his facility at drawing and devising experimental proofs for theoretical problems. His main 'subjects' were anatomy, astronomy and gnomics (the study of sun dials). His illustrations for Dr Willis's book *Anatomy of the Brain* were much admired (*Plate 49*) and the geometrical figure he produced as a partial solution to an arithmetical problem posed by Pascal (in 1658) was warmly applauded by the French thinker.

Wren took his BA in 1650 and his MA in 1653, becoming a Fellow of All Souls in the same year. In 1657 he was appointed Professor of Astronomy at Gresham College, London, returning to Oxford in 1661 to become Savilian Professor of Astronomy. Wren's colleagues at Wadham and Gresham College thought of themselves as 'experimental philosophers', which nicely epitomizes the mixture of abstract and practical thinking involved in their work (*Plate 50*).

Wren's friend Robert Hooke, who had had a similar education at Westminster and Oxford (Christ Church), came to an interest in architecture by a very similar combination of practical and theoretical skills. His judgement on Wren could also be applied to himself: 'Since the time of Archimedes, there scarce ever met in one man, in so great a perfection, such a mechanical hand, and so philosophical a Mind.' (*Micrographia,* 1665.) The picture we have of Wren in 1660 is one of an already eminent and much admired member of an advanced circle of rational thinkers, who combined a sceptical attitude to religious dogma and superstition with a passion for mathematical certainties. Contact with Puritans in Oxford seems to have counteracted the Laudian background of his father and uncle. We have seen how Hobbes wrote: 'When a man Reasoneth, he does nothing else but conceive a summe totall, from Addition of parcels; or conceive a Remainder, from Substraction of one summe from another . . .' (*Leviathan,* p 110). Wren used similar terminology in his inaugural lecture as Savilian Professor of Astronomy: 'Therefore it would be right to call mathematics rather than logic the instrument of instruments of all the more certain sciences . . . only mathematical demonstrations built on the immovable foundation of geometry and arithmetic attain insuperable truth . . .' (Quoted in Sekler *Wren and his place in European Architecture,* p 35.) We would expect such a man to take a keen interest in the practical and structural aspects of architecture, but it would be less easy to see how he would respond to the problem of style. Later, when he came to write about beauty in architecture, he was to recognize that part of architectural aesthetics depended on custom and tradition. But, he declared, 'always the true test is natural or geometrical beauty'.

He did not resign his Professorship until 1673, but, as early as 1663, Wren's absences from Oxford were being noticed with disapproval. London was the place to be, with the moves to found the Royal Society gathering momentum, and the interested attentions of Charles II to be catered for. Wren prepared lectures and experiments for the group which was meeting regularly at Gresham College, and was asked by the King to carry out some microscopical drawings of insects and a model of the moon. In 1661, Charles asked Wren to supervise the fortification of Tangier, acquired as a result of the marriage of Catherine of Braganza. As an incentive, the King took the surprising step of offering the thirty year old scientist the reversion of Sir John Denham's position as Surveyor General. Although Wren declined this offer, the King was to remain convinced that Wren was the man to run his Office of Works, and indeed gave him the job when Denham eventually went mad and died in 1669.

Despite the claims of May, Pratt and Webb for the position of Surveyor General, Wren could clearly be seen as a front runner, since by 1669 he had already designed a number of buildings and been allotted key roles in the rebuilding of London and St Paul's. But in 1661, Wren had yet to design a single building, although there is evidence that he had shown his scientific colleagues some 'new designs tending to strength, convenience and beauty in buildings' in 1660. We must assume that these inventions were of the learned and theoretical kind which we would expect in a circle which included knowledgeable men in architectural matters such as John Evelyn. What turned Wren the experimental philosopher into the nation's most famous architect was the pressing demand for new building and the commissions of his University colleagues and the Court.

The stepping stones between Wren's first essays in architectural design in 1661 and his assumption of the mantle of Surveyor General in 1669 can be briefly tabulated:

1663	Designed the Sheldonian Theatre, Oxford, a gift of Archbishop Sheldon (erstwhile Fellow of All Souls).
	Consulted by the Commission for the repair of Old St Paul's. He later produced a report and a design, just before the Fire, in 1666.
1664–5	A design for a new Whitehall Palace for Charles II probably belongs to this period.
1665–6	Wren travels to France, to meet scientists and study the architecture of the King and his courtiers. This trip was crucial to Wren's development as an architect.
c. 1665–9	Two designs which cannot be dated precisely, but which led to the following buildings: 1668–73, Emmanuel College Cambridge, chapel and gallery. 1668, Trinity College Oxford, north wing of the garden quadrangle.
1668	Report on the structural condition of Salisbury Cathedral for the Bishop, his friend, Dr Seth Ward, who had preceded him as Savilian Professor of Astronomy.

Wren's real chance came with the Fire. He was quick to present the King with a wildly optimistic project for the complete replanning of the City, along with a number of other proposals by men like John Evelyn. These are discussed in Television programme 12. The King appointed him, Pratt and May as the three Surveyors for the Royal Commission for the rebuilding of London. The City appointed Mills, Jerman and Hooke to their parallel committee, and between them they prepared the 1667 Rebuilding Act which was to govern the reconstruction of the City.

By then, Wren was the Surveyor General, and consequently entrusted with the design of all new buildings administered by the Office of Works. Meanwhile, the Dean of St Paul's, another old friend, William Sancroft, was determined to see that Wren was put in charge of the reconstruction of the now utterly ruined cathedral. It was in a sense fortunate for Wren that the emergency repairs carried out in 1666–7 proved unstable, and that the Dutch war prevented any firm decisions until Wren's appointment as Surveyor. As it turned out, then, a whole list of Wren's friends in high places were, for different reasons, determined to see Wren given the Surveyorship. Charles's decision appears less mysterious.

Robert Hooke (1635–1703)

Hooke's career followed that of Wren rather closely. After an early apprenticeship as a painter to Peter Lely, where he found the smell of paint unbearable, Hooke went to Westminster under Dr Busby, just a few years behind Wren. He showed an outstanding early aptitude for geometry and mathematics. In 1653, he progressed to Christ Church, Oxford, taking his BA in 1658 and his MA in 1663. He became a close friend to Wren and a loyal attender at the meetings of the Experimental Philosophical Club, where he excelled in the development of microscopes, telescopes, watches and the full range of chemical, physical and experimental activities of the group. Hooke's scientific discoveries were probably much more important than Wren's, on a practical as well as a theoretical level.

As an architect, Hooke was content to remain in the shadow of Wren, with whom he regularly discussed the theory and history of architecture. He was ready in 1666 to present his own plan for a rebuilt London to the King after the Fire, and the Court of Common Council of the City accepted it, declaring that they greatly preferred it to that of the City Surveyor, Mills. It was presumably his reputation as a scientist, and the fact that many of the city fathers attended the lectures at Gresham College which led to his appointment as one of the City's Surveyors for the rebuilding of the City. The salary of £150 was a much needed boost to Hooke's finances.

It is now clear that Hooke made designs for a large number of buildings in the sixteen-seventies and eighties, although few were built and almost none survive today. Ramsbury Manor, Wiltshire (*Plates 14, 15, 82*) is an elegant house in the tradition of Pratt and May, and the church Hooke built for Dr Busby (Willen, Bucks) is a worthy exercise in the new style. His most spectacular building, Bethlehem Hospital, Moorfields (*Plates 52–3*), was demolished in the nineteenth century, as was his Royal College of Physicians – two examples which perfectly express the influence of French and Dutch architecture respectively in his work.

We have looked at a range of people who practised architecture (the design of buildings) in the seventeenth century. We have seen that their social and cultural backgrounds were diverse, but that they shared a common approach to architecture. Many of them had travelled abroad, or were aware of foreign architecture from books. The influence of Dutch examples was clearly important for domestic architecture of all kinds. We will see, however, that French influences were more significant for the kind of ambitious projects which Wren was called on to tackle by Charles II.

Christopher Wren and Stuart cultural policy

We will have to begin by asking the question, 'Did the Restoration mark a return to the cultural policy of Charles I?' We're going to come to a similar conclusion as that which J. R. Jones and Christopher Hill have already given to similar political and constitutional questions. There is a strong continuity, but the changes brought about by the Interregnum were substantial and largely irreversible. We will find that some of the projects closest to Charles I's heart, such as a grandiloquent palace in Whitehall and a renovation of St Paul's, are still much discussed in the corridors of power. There were more politically unpopular buildings, including lavish apartments and chapels for a Catholic Queen and a Catholic Queen Mother. After the exclusion crisis, there was even a half-built Royal Palace, in a French style, paid for out of secret service funds reputed to come from Louis XIV. Architecture was still in the dangerously controversial zone of Stuart public imagery. And even Clarendon went too far, with the magnificent house Roger Pratt designed for him in Piccadilly (*Plate 13*). A contemporary libel gets the popular reaction right:

> Here lie the consecrated bones
> Of Paules, late gelded of his stones
> Here lies the golden briberies,
> The price of ruined families
> The cavaliers debenter wall
>   Built in the eccentric Basis
> Here's Dunkirk Town and Tangier hall,
> The marriage of the Queen and all,
>   The Dutchman's *Templum Pacis*

(Quoted in Gunther *The Architecture of Sir Roger Pratt*.)

The records show that Pratt did buy some of his stone from St Paul's, but whether Clarendon really built his house out of the proceeds of nonconformist fines, bribes, the Portuguese marriage treaty or the sale of Dunkirk is less certain although it became quite widely known as Dunkirk House, and was seen to represent the power of over-mighty rulers. The house was barely finished when, according to Pepys, some 'rude people' vandalised the property, setting up a gibbet with the words 'Three sights to be seen, Dunkirk, Tangier and a barren Queen'. After Clarendon's disgrace and exile, the house changed hands several times and was finally sold for demolition to a consortium of bankers under the leadership of Sir Thomas Bond (hence Bond Street) who proposed to develop the property to the north of Piccadilly. The house was demolished in 1683, the first of the new great houses along Piccadilly to give way to the soaring land prices which the spread of the west end were to generate in the eighteenth century. A consortium of city bankers developed the site, including what is now Bond Street.

Charles was more tactful. He may have learnt a political lesson from the effect of Clarendon's sumptuous house on public opinion. The new buildings at Newmarket and, in the sixteen-eighties, Winchester, were well out of the public eye. The projected palace at Greenwich was given a relatively low priority and left unfinished at his death. It is a key feature of the period that most of the great buildings were truly State offices like the Customs House, rather than royal monuments. The City churches and St Paul's were paid for out of a tax on coals voted by Parliament. Ironically, it was William III who was able to complete the most splendid Royal Palace for himself, with Wren's additions to Hampton Court. And Wren's completion of Greenwich, under William and Mary, was as a naval hospital rather than as a Royal Palace. It is undoubtedly true that Chelsea Hospital was modelled on Louis XIV's foundation of the Invalides in Paris, but Wren's building is a markedly more discreet edifice than the French one. Charles was reluctant to risk his independence from Parliament during the sixteen-eighties by bankrupting himself with building projects, and James quickly stopped work on Winchester for the same reason.

French influences in Court architecture

There is little doubt that Wren admired the architecture of the French Renaissance and Baroque. His visit to the Paris area in 1665–6 enabled him to study these buildings at first hand. Robert Hooke, too, was a keen student of French architecture and their friend John Evelyn was considered an expert in the field, translating the controversial treatise by Fréart de Chambray, the *Parallèle*, soon after its French publication. The main features of French architecture which attracted these men were its sophisticated and subtle handling of decoration.

Most French buildings of this period were considerably more ornate than comparable English examples. In particular, French Renaissance architecture almost always treated wall surfaces as planes to be modelled and subdivided. The *cour carré* of the Louvre (*Plate 51*), begun in 1546 by Pierre

Lescot and continued by Lemercier in 1624, set the standard for French architectural sculpture. Although few English architects seem to have been attracted to this scale of decoration, many French details evident here do occur in English architectural decoration. The round or oval window, or relief panel, framed by a festoon which flows down on either side, for instance, will crop up later. And the French preference for large segmental pediments full of sculpture also feature in some buildings. Robert Hooke's Bethlehem Hospital (*Plates 52–3*) reveals a rather French roof silhouette and a taste at least of French decorative sculpture. The biggest challenge posed by the French was the sheer richness of the treatment, and the insistent use of the classical orders. Le Vau's chateau at Vaux-le-Vicomte (1657–61) (*Plates 54–5*), could be described in terms which compare it to Pratt's Clarendon House (*Plate 13*) – at least there is a portico in the middle of the facade and a form of 'H' plan. Le Vau realized the ideal of this kind of classical architecture by placing a great oval hall under a dome in the centre of one of the facades. And his use of a giant order of pilasters renders the whole design extremely 'elevated' in classical terms. Again, there were no takers for this scale of magnificence in England, but several of the details were imitated.

The Office of Works

During Denham's Surveyorship (1660–9), the main building works were the King's House at Newmarket, on which around £8,000 were spent, the beginning of a Royal Palace at Greenwich and the purchase and repair of Audley End. Newmarket was designed by William Samwell, a gentleman architect of some distinction. The mediaeval house which Inigo Jones had extended had been almost completely destroyed during the Interregnum, and Samwell's new building provided only modest accommodation for the King's and the Duke of York's households. Greenwich was begun to Webb's design, but only one block was built (*Plates 69–71*).

Webb probably also had a hand in the remodelling of Somerset House (*Plate 56*) for the Queen Dowager, Henrietta Maria. The most famous part of this work was the new gallery wing probably by Webb, containing a Presence Chamber and Privy Chamber. The design is so close to the style of Inigo Jones that the commonly held attribution – that Webb made use of a design by his master – has some credibility. A high rusticated basement with a giant order of pilasters framing two storeys derives directly from Italian Renaissance prototypes. It is interesting to note that Wren turned to a very similar treatment for his proposed 'Piazza' which would have surrounded St Paul's (*Plate 57*). And at least one other building, the Marquess of Worcester's house Badminton, Gloucestershire (*c.* 1666) was remodelled in direct imitation of Somerset House Gallery.

Under Denham the Office of Works did not exercise any particular authority in stylistic terms, since the Surveyor was forced to turn to other experts to design the Royal buildings. The main tendency was in the direction of a revival of Jonesian Palladianism, and the presence of Edward Marshall as Master Mason would certainly have supported this direction.

The Custom House

One of the few buildings undertaken by the Office of Works during the sixteen-seventies was the Custom House (*Plate 58*), which had been burnt in the Fire. Wren was first involved in his capacity as Surveyor for the rebuilding of London, helping to sort out the tangled property rights on the site of the new building. Before he became Surveyor, plans had been prepared for the Customs farmers, which they presented to the Treasury for construction. But before anything could be done, Wren succeeded to the Surveyorship and quickly intervened to veto the proposed plans. His own plans entailed an expenditure of another £3,000, but this was approved by the Lords of the Treasury and work began in June, 1669.

The building benefited from a judgement of the Fire Court,[1] which gave it a new site facing the river. Wren's plan exploits this frontage, with a main block and two wings. The main block contained one great room on the upper level, for the transaction of public business, while the wings included the minor offices and reception rooms. Maximum freedom of access at ground level was ensured by lifting the body of the building on piers. This gives the building a curiously squat proportion, since the lower story is neither treated as a massive basement nor as an equal to the upper. A more correct handling would have been to follow the model of Webb's Somerset House Gallery (Plate 56), or a similar treatment. In detail, the Custom House reveals every sign of Dutch influence, with the stone swags applied as decoration above the windows. The building cost just over £10,000, paid for out of the customs duties, and was finished in 1671. By 1698, the accommodation was already much too small to deal with the increased volume of trade, and piecemeal extensions were required.

Wren and the restoration of Jonesian ideals

A case can be made to see Wren as a royal architect comparable to Jones in the formulation of a propagandist Court style. Just as Jones had designed a catafalque for James I, for instance, (see Block 2, p 26), so Wren drew up Italianate designs for a mausoleum for Charles I in 1678, after Parliament had voted £70,000 for the purpose (Plates 59–61). Grinling Gibbons also designed a monument for the mausoleum (Plate 39). However, the money did not materialize and nothing came of the project; but this lavish design, if built, would have formed a clear testimonial to the survival of absolutist dynastic aspirations during the Restoration. As in the case of Jones's catafalque, the design used a version of the dome of St Peter's, Rome, and a body based on Bramante's Tempietto in Rome. An influential French example would have been the Valois mausoleum designed at St Denis a century earlier (Plate 62), or Louis XIV's planned mausoleum of 1676, which became the Invalides chapel. Wren's mausoleum would have been built at Windsor, and would have been simply the most explicit of a series of grandiose projects which were transforming the old castle.

Windsor Castle

Windsor was where Charles I had been buried, and the Castle was a fortified garrison with three companies of troops on hand (Plate 63). Whether Charles II thought of it as a Rocca – a last redoubt – to escape to if things got rough, or whether he thought of it as the symbolic heart of Stuart pomp and circumstance, it was here that he decided to spend most money on repairs and renovations. Early work was mostly concerned with strengthening the defences of the fortress, under Constable Mordaunt and Prince Rupert (Constable after 1668). Wren had particular associations with Windsor, since his father and uncle before him had been Registrars of the Order of the Garter, whose seat was in St George's Hall, Windsor. Wren himself had been entrusted with the records of the Order during the Interregnum, and handed them over personally to the King at the Restoration. But the main work of improving Windsor Castle for State ceremonials was given to Hugh May, as part recompense for being passed over as Surveyor. In 1673, May was made Comptroller of the works at Windsor at a specially generous salary of £500 and it was only after his death that Wren added this job to his list of appointments. In 1674, funds were found to begin a complete reconstruction of part of the Upper Ward, to provide suites of apartments and state rooms for the King and Queen and a reconstruction of the chapel and St George's Hall. Over £150,000 seems to have been spent on these works between 1674

---

[1]For the role of the Fire Court in settling disputes after the Fire, see Broadcast Notes for Television programme 12.

and 1685. The money came from a variety of Royal revenues, including £18,000 from Louis XIV's subsidy and, in the last phase, £1,000 a month of Irish revenue.

Verrio's ceilings (*Plate 64*) carried out a full-blooded exposition of Stuart absolutism, comparable in content, if not in pictorial quality, to Rubens's ceiling at the Banqueting House. Antonio Verrio was brought to England especially for this kind of work. The Privy Chamber ceiling, for example, portrayed:

> A most lively representation of the re-establishment of the Church of England, on the restoration of Charles 2nd in the Characters of England, Scotland and Ireland attended by Faith, Hope and Charity, Religion triumphing over Superstitions and Hypocrisy, who are driven by Cupids from the face of the Church.
>
> (Quoted by Colvin, *The History of the King's Works,* V, p 322.)

In the Great Bedchamber, France is shown with the four continents as suppliants bringing gifts to Charles II – rather ironic given the £18,000 worth of French money invested in the Windsor buildings. In the Queen's apartments, Catherine of Braganza received similarly pompous treatment (*Plate 64*). The redecoration of the King's Chapel was not begun in earnest until 1680–2. Verrio's painted scenes covered ceiling and upper walls, and Grinling Gibbons was given a chance to show off in virtuoso mouldings, carved seats and stalls and sprays of palm leaves, laurels and fruit. At the same time, St George's Hall (*Plate 83*) was redecorated with the Garter ceremonial occasions, with gilded plasterwork, paintings and carvings. Charles II was depicted in glory in the centre of the ceiling, while other paintings and relief panels treated the iconography of St George.

Whitehall Palace

Windsor was the nearest Charles II came to creating a real Versailles for his family to display itself to courtiers and foreign potentates. It was safely out of the eye of lower echelon courtiers and Members of Parliament. Charles had not given up hope of his father's great ambition, completely to rebuild the Palace of Whitehall. Webb and Wren both produced drawings in the early sixties, but a major designing effort by Wren after the fire which wrecked the Palace in 1698 came to nothing, partly from the prudence of William III and partly from his asthmatic condition which rendered the site intolerable to him. William's palace was to be Hampton Court, not Whitehall. That these schemes had little real hope of being carried out is attested by the amount of money spent patching up the old palace, building new ranges for the King and Queen and countless minor additions for members of the royal family, the royal mistresses and to cater for hobbies of the King, such as a laboratory, tennis court, aviary and so on. Under James II, a new range was added facing the Privy Garden, including another Catholic chapel (in addition to Jones's chapel in St James's Palace) and a new council chamber. James spent over £35,000 in his brief reign on these additions to Whitehall, and the splendidly adorned new chapel, where the King and Queen first heard mass openly at Christmas 1686, did nothing to allay the suspicions of Court or city. Almost all these additions were destroyed in the fire of 1698. The subsequent history of the Catholic altar, with its carvings by Gibbons and Arnold Quellin, has already been indicated.

Charles's flirtation with a complete rebuilding of the old Palace of Whitehall is known to have continued at least until 1664, when Evelyn recounts that the King 'designed to me the plot for the future building of Whitehall, together with the rooms of state'. A dated drawing by John Webb, from 1661, outlines a plan for a massive new palace similar to the one he had designed for Charles I, in 1647, following Jones's general scheme. Soon afterwards, however, Webb set about preparing detailed plans and elevations of a much smaller palace (*Plates 65–7*). Two drawings by Wren depict elevations which fit with a plan of this configuration, and at least one of these must be from Charles' reign, since the crossed 'C's are shown in the decoration (*Plate 68*). In each of these schemes, the idea was to use the existing Banqueting House, add another similar building and create a great frontispiece in the middle. On the St James's Park side, two courts would contain apartments for the King and Queen, and State rooms, while two ranges leading down to the river would include the subsidiary apartments and service rooms. Charles seems to have used this project to test out the architectural skills of Webb, Wren and May (a drawing has been tentatively attributed to May for a similar scheme). Wren's drawing betrays a number of rather fiddly decorative details, while Webb's scheme shows a confident mastery of the giant order – his central temple front portico and side pavilions would have introduced a splendid foil to the delicate textures and rhythms of Inigo Jones's Banqueting Hall.

Greenwich Palace

Webb's design relates closely to his first schemes for Greenwich Palace (*Plates 69–71*). Here the basic principles of Baroque palace design are reduced to their simplest and most effective form. A few bold accents are linked by rows of windows set in channelled masonry. Each wing resembles Webb's earlier designs for Belvoir Castle (*Plate 72*), *c*. 1655. Crowning the Greenwich Palace composition would have been a grand circular hall capped with a dome – the prestigious feature which French architects had frequently used. Webb's scheme would have blocked the view to the Queen's House, but when Wren came to complete the building, as a naval hospital (1694) he too produced a design with a similar, even more imposing centrepiece. Eventually, however, this idea was abandoned in favour of the present arrangement, with two parallel ranges flanking a vista from the Queen's House to the river.

Winchester Palace

But Wren did design a palace which carried out the basic theme of Webb's design. This was Winchester Palace, begun in 1682 and left unfinished at Charles's death. Charles seems to have conceived the idea for this palace somewhat precipitously, since he appears never to have visited Winchester before 1682. The palace was intended to be more than a hunting lodge on the lines of Newmarket. The plan (*Plates 73–4*) followed the general lines of Webb's Greenwich with the important difference that the Court is stepped back in two stages. This was the arrangement chosen by Louis XIV and Le Vau for the enlargement of Versailles, and the French connection must be taken seriously here. Apart from the French subsidies which made the whole project possible, Winchester was conveniently close to the coast and far enough from London to make diplomatic contacts with the French safe. The Palace contained two chapels, one Anglican and one Catholic, and provision was being made to buy the land between the palace and the Cathedral, which would have created a monumental axis through the town. The central feature (*Plate 75*) was not a dome, but a French-style mansard roof, over a great staircase. Subsidiary cupolas over the two chapels, which formed the projections into the inner court and a grand central portico would have contributed to a reasonably imposing composition. The craftsmen used were all men heavily involved with the city churches and St Paul's, which is a tribute to the resources these men could bring to bear on an emergency building campaign, rushed through in three years almost to completion. £44,623 was spent before James II called a final halt to the work. It is not clear how much of this money came from the secret supply from Louis XIV, but it is likely that the Palace would not have been started without some such source.

The other great project of Royal munificence in the sixteen-eighties was Chelsea Hospital (1682) (*Plates 76–8*). The importance of Louis's foundation at the Invalides has already been mentioned. Drawings of this building were sent to the Duke of Monmouth in 1678. The Royal Hospital was not paid for by the Exchequer and did not formally come under Wren's authority in the Office of Works. But it was natural that he should be given the job of designing and supervising its construction. Sir Stephen Fox, Paymaster General of the army, promoted the project, and started a fund based on army pay deductions. This was supplemented by the Privy Purse. Wren borrowed the basic idea of Webb's small Whitehall scheme, placing a grand temple front portico between two large halls. Two wings formed a court open to the river, each wing accented by an applied portico in the centre. The stark contrast between these large stone porticos and the absolutely plain brick walls and white windows of the dormitories lends great power to the design. This, more than Winchester, was a genuinely innovatory, and very English, interpretation of continental palace designs. Instead of a dome over the main portico, Wren placed a curiously delicate lantern. While lacking the pomp of the Invalides, or the later schemes for Greenwich, the effect is surprisingly successful. Wren was eminently pragmatic; Chelsea Hospital provides the maximum well lit and ventilated accommodation for the pensioners, combined with a dignified monumentality, at the least price.

The story of Wren's work for the Office of Works under Charles II and James II is not merely a question of listing the big schemes, executed and unexecuted. Much of the daily routine of measuring, surveying, repairing and estimating is recorded in the documents but difficult to visualize. Wren's ability to build up a team of professional clerks and draughtsmen stood him in good stead as he himself became older and his responsibilities increased. Much of his greatest work was to follow the Glorious Revolution, and it would not have been possible without the collaboration of men like Dickinson, Hawksmoor and Vanbrugh who played an important role in the completion of Greenwich and the final stages of St Paul's.

Conclusion

In a sense, Greenwich Hospital (*Plate 79*) seems to sum up the history of monumental architecture under the Stuarts. Inigo Jones's Queen's House was specifically Italian in style (Palladian, to be precise). The house was a personal property for the Queen. If Charles II had persevered with Webb's palace design, the image of Stuart autocracy would have achieved specific focus in a public building. As a naval hospital, however, under William and Mary, and in the fully fledged baroque style of Wren's last period, the building became a symbol of state power, rather than Stuart absolutism.

The baroque was a short lived style in Britain, to be replaced after 1715 by another revival, more pedantic this time, of the forms and principles of Palladio's architecture. The great Whig Palladian villas of the eighteenth century would destroy the subtle balance of good craftsmanship and informal, but well proportioned, architectural composition which we have been looking at. The eighteenth century would mark the final victory of the professional architect, complete with text book treatises, over the collaborative efforts of gentleman amateurs, builders, sculptors and intellectuals.

References

Colvin, H. (ed) (1975–) *The History of the King's Works,* Vol III–IV, HMSO.
Colvin, H. (1978) *A Biographical Dictionary of British Architects,* John Murray.
Gunther, R. T. (ed) (1979) *The Architecture of Sir Roger Pratt,* Arno.
Owens, W. R. (ed) (1980) *Seventeenth-century England: A Changing Culture,* Vol 2, *Modern Studies,* Ward Lock. (Reader)
Sekler, E. F. (1956) *Wren and his place in European Architecture,* Faber.
Summerson, J. (1969) *Architecture in Britain 1530 to 1830,* Pelican.

Seventeenth-century England: A Changing Culture, 1618–1689